MEDICAL BILLING

The Bottom Line

Claudia A. Yalden

BORDERLANDS PRESS
Grantham ☐ 1997

MEDICAL BILLING: THE BOTTOM LINE
Copyright © 1997 by Claudia A. Yalden
All rights reserved

This publication is designed to provide accurate and authoritative information with regard to the subject matter covered. It is sold with the understanding that the author is not engaged in rendering legal, accounting, or other professional advice. If legal advice or other expert assistance is required, the services of a qualified professional person should be sought.
—*From a Declaration of Principles jointly adapted by a Committee of the American Bar Association and a Committee of Publishers and Associations.*

No part of this publication may be reproduced or transmitted in any form or by any means, electronic or mechanical, including photocopy, recording, or any information storage and retrieval system, without explicit permission in writing from the Author.

To order additional copies call 1-800-221-0488

ISBN # 1-880325-39-X

Library of Congress # 97-070269

Cover design by Claudia A. Yalden
Typesetting by Elizabeth E. Monteleone

Printed and bound in the United States of America

Borderlands Press
PO Box 1524
Grantham NH 03753
603-863-9879; fax 603-863-9888

This book is dedicated to my wonderful husband for his support, both financially and mentally. He has been by my side from the beginning. And to my children whose encouragement kept me focused.

And I cannot fail to mention my sincere thanks to Marsha Simmons and my cousin Bo Plant for all their editing, and to Michael Lane who freed up my time.

In addition, I will never forget all my billing buddies, Bruce Wade, Sally Fulton, Jo-Anne Sheehan, Lois Friedman, Peggy Kozy and Beverly Gushikuma for all their help and support.

And to Elizabeth and Tom Monteleone who pushed me to the finish line. Without their push and determination this book would still be sitting in my computer.

Contents

Introduction — 7

Chapter 1 — 11
  The Bottom Line

Chapter 2 — 15
  Obtaining Financial Help

Chapter 3 — 19
  Setting Up Your Home Office

Chapter 4 — 23
  The Business Plan

Chapter 5 — 25
  Writing A Business Plan
  Facts About a Small Business

Chapter 6 — 31
  Getting Started and Networking

Chapter 7 — 33
  Buzz Words—Superbills—Claim Forms

Chapter 8 — 35
  Reference Books

Chapter 9 — 43
  What Doctors Wants to Hear

Chapter 10 — 49
  Pricing Your Services
  and Cost Projections

Chapter 11 — 57
  Marketing Strategies

Chapter 12   59
    Cold Calling

Chapter 13   61
    Newspapers:
    Following the Help Wanted Ads

Chapter 14   65
    Direct Marketing:
    Press Releases—Hospital—Advertising

Chapter 15   69
    Postcards & Brochures

Chapter 16   79
    Letters & Marketing Techniques

Chapter 17   93
    Packets & What to Include

Chapter 18   107
    The Presentation Packet

Chapter 19   115
    Contracts & Forms

Chapter 20   123
    Software and Its Cost

Chapter 21   135
    Clarifying the Alphabet Soup of
    Managed Care

Chapter 22   139
    Common Questions & Answers

You Cannot Discover New Oceans

Unless You Have The Courage

To Lose Sight Of The Shore

— *Successories*, 1996

Introduction

My Message to You . . .

Many people and forces helped me make this book possible. It was designed and written to help the many people who are interested in the medical and dental billing business and don't know where to begin. I was there once . . . and found out there is no ready reference books available.

I feel this book will tell you that everything is possible and I thank my parents, Mildred and Pierre Becker, who made me possible. The first page and the last pages could not have been written without the loving support and tolerance of my special husband, Robert, and my determination to be with my grandson Patrick. They were literally by my side throughout the process. And a special thanks for the ongoing encouragement of my two sons Robert and Jeffrey who encouraged me from the beginning and told me I could do it and to my daughter Christin.

A special thanks goes out to Jo-Anne Sheehan whose encouragement and professional ideas helped me finish and put my ideas into writing. It was through this book that Jo-Anne became my "very dear friend." And a special thanks to Lou, Beverly, Bruce, Lois, Sheena, Sally and all my Prodigy friends for all their inspiration, ideas, help, and most of all their support.

As you travel through this book learning how you too can be an entreprenuer and fulfill your dreams you will see where I made mistakes which cost me thousands of dollars. After many questions and problems I decided that a book needed to be written . . . to help people who, like me, wanted to get into this business without spending a lot of money.

I started my medical billing business to get out of the rat race of commuting to Boston and to be with my grandson, Patrick. I always wanted to be an entrepreneur and thought the medical billing business was just what I wanted. I was away from billing for over 10 years, but I felt having a background working in the Child Development Unit at Children's Hospital in Boston with Dr. Terry B. Brazelton would be an asset and a credit that would allow me to easily get started. I never realized how changes and time affected billing. Just as television, the greatest invention of its time was sold in black and white and later went on to be sold in color, so is the medical billing business. Claims were once submitted. Doctors were paid. Secondary insurance was filed. There was no capitation, adjustments, write-offs, managed care and there was no medigap.

This book is designed to give you the knowledge to get started in the electronic medical billing industry; ideas on financial help; equipment needed; and office operation suggestions. Through my experience of failures and successes, and the knowledge I've gained from so many people, I have decided to share with you ideas of marketing strategies. For the new entrepreneur I introduce books, organizations, and reputable vendors that will help you on your way. Also, you'll read some true experiences and common questions with answers that many people need to know.

This book is written as a layman's manual, giving ideas of the basic "nuts and bolts" of the business and hopefully assisting you in your decision. Is this right for me? My desire is for you to gain insight toward financial benefit of a business like this, using cost comparison charts along with how to price your services. Last but not least, I refer to many areas concerning medical software. My hope is for you to understand what is needed, the pitfalls you may face, and how to succeed from the beginning.

Although all your questions will not be answered, it is the beginning of learning the business. There are still many experts in the field who may be able to help you. However, if you cannot find the answer to your questions, please feel free to contact me and I will assist you in finding someone who can help. I needed the support and used it. My new goal is to help support you.

**Good luck in your business,
and remember . . .
don't give up!**

*Claudia A Yalden
New Hampshire
January 1997*

Chapter 1

The Bottom Line . . .

Let's face it . . . everyone today wants to go into business, become the entrepreneur of the 21st century, and become independently wealthy or maybe comfortable. They want to pay off their bills, send their children to college, drive the car of their dreams, vacation in the sun, and have a bank account where you don't have to balance it. Or maybe you just want some extra income to supplement what you already have, or possibly you want something to fall back on in retirement. Whatever your reasons . . . you have decided you want to investigate **Medical or Dental Electronic Billing.**

Although electronic claims submission is growing . . . it still has a long way to go. The market is huge.

Each year the percentage of electronic claims being filed is growing. Although it is encouraging, let's look at the other side of this coin. Each year more and more practices are being bought out by the big, powerful HMO's, PPO's, etc. That could possibly mean they will have their own capability to file their claims electronically and have no need for you, or . . . they could realize the benefits of outsourcing and you may be lucky to land the account. The bottom line I would like to stress to you is this is a very tough, hard, business. You will not get rich quickly, and if that is the reason you are contemplating going into this business, then I suggest you save your money. This business WILL TAKE TIME, PERSEVERANCE, AND PERSISTENCE. You need to market and you need to be determined not to quit, not to get discouraged and you need to follow a marketing plan faithfully. Only when you can commit to that will you be able to make money and know that this business will work . .. but *"it will take time."*

So . . . if you're still contemplating going into the Medical and Dental Billing business, I will share my ideas on how to market, give an example of how to write a business plan, and suggest a direction on how to market. When I began this business I thought that I should only target my market on the small town family doctors or narrow in on the specialties that were not part of an HMO, PPO. Years later my thoughts changed because even doctors that are part of an HMO, or PPO, etc. are in need of your service. Doctors in a big medical/dental center are in need of your service. There are some big opportunities out there and if you don't try and market them, someone else will. Ambulance companies and Durable Medical Equipment suppliers are great to target in on. Very few ambulance companies utilize electronic billing and all the advantages that go with it. Durable Medical Equipment is an entirely different kind of billing but they too have to submit claims for wheelchairs, walkers, crutches, ostomy supplies, etc. Don't overlook any opportunity.

Businesses fail because the majority of small business owners have a work mentality, not a business mentality. In this business you will need both. You will continually have to educate yourself by joining organizations and reading everything available to keep abreast of the continuing changes. You need to contact your Medicare/Medicaid office in your state. Get on their mailing list and tell them you want to be notified of any seminars coming up. Call your Blue Cross/Blue Shield office. They too offer seminars. And the best part of these seminars are that they are generally free. Check with the local hospitals for seminars they sponsor. Attend as many as you possibility can.

You can make money in this business but I cannot emphasize enough that —

"the name of the game is perseverance."

I have outlined the basics of getting started, marketing, obtaining software and pricing your services. After that, it is up to you.

There are many organizations to join which I've listed in chapter 21.

Call these organizations to get a copy of the newsletters. I feel these organizations will keep you well informed. One organization (NACAP) offers a two-day training seminar and a yearly conference at various locations around the country in which NACAP members receive a reduced rate.

Once you decide to become involved in this business you will become a Claims Processor. You will also be receiving constant updates from your software vendor or clearinghouse. You will be providing electronic claims submission for physicians and other health care providers and you will be soaring to new heights in your development and career.

CHAPTER 2

OBTAINING FINANCIAL HELP

There are many agencies willing to give grants. A lot of these grants do not have to be paid back.

You can obtain information on grants from the local library or with programs such as Prodigy, America-On-Line, CompuServe, and the Internet. If you don't have access to one of these programs, I suggest you inquire at a local computer store about purchasing the software or call:

Prodigy (1-800-PRODIGY),
America-On-Line (1-800-827-6364),
CompuServe (1-800-343-8913).

These programs offer free software along with free hours for first time users. Prodigy, America-On-Line and CompuServe all have a medical billing bulletin board and you will find a lot of billers hang out there. I personally hang out on Prodigy. There is a wealth of information you can gather from other billers who belong to these on-line services. A book worth reading on obtaining grants is ***The Action Guide to Government Grants, Loans, and Giveaways,*** by George Chelekis which is a comprehensive guide to getting millions of dollars in grants, loan guarantees, loans, and other financial help from federal and state government sources. It is well worth the $24.95 investment or borrow it from your local library.

The entire government grant and loan awards process has, in the past, gotten a bad rap from the media. They probably deserved it since not only were taxpayer dollars wasted, but the projects funded just didn't make sense. Government and private funding were being used for such things as a quick-cooked hamburger that cooks in less than 30 seconds with no smoke and no pre-heating of the grill. It's no wonder they received a bad rap!

There are certain guidelines which need to be followed if you are to obtain a loan or grant:

They are:

- ✔ a financial statement includes a balance sheet and a profit and loss statement;
- ✔ a resume of management and brief history of the business;
- ✔ loan proposal, outlining the use of proceeds of the loan and maturity needed and,
- ✔ a one year profit and loss projection.

For additional information, contact the **U.S. SMALL BUSINESS ADMINISTRATION** at **800-8-ASK-SBA** and ask for the number of your local SBA office. You can also obtain information on any of the following sources:

- SBA District Offices
- Small Business Development Centers (SBDCs)
- Service Corps of Retired Executives (SCORE)
- Small Business Institutes (SBIs)

SBA offers small business loans of $100,000 or less. They guarantee up to 90% of the loan. You can get a response within 2 or 3 days. Interest rates cannot exceed SBA maximums and the length of time for repayment depends on your ability to repay, the use of the loan proceeds and may not exceed 25 years for fixed assets or 10 years for all other uses. You will need a current business balance sheet, a profit and loss statement, personal financial statement and a list of collateral to be offered.

SCORE is a 13,000 member volunteer program sponsored by the SBA. They offer management counseling and training for small businesses and to those considering going into business. They also offer pre-business workshops as well as a variety of other workshops nationwide to prospective small business entrepreneurs. Among other things, they have training and educational programs, advisory services, publications, financial programs and contract assistance. They specialize in programs for women business owners, minorities, veterans, international trade and rural development.

Chapter 3

Setting Up Your Home Office

It goes without saying that a computer is your primary tool. If you already have a computer, you're ready to take the dive and go into business. Most software is for an IBM clone but there are a few companies who sell for MacIntosh as well. You will also need a printer, modem, and a dedicated phone line with an answering machine. Most computers come with a built-in fax/modem. If your computer does not have a built-in modem you will have to buy an external modem. Looking in second-hand stores (especially second-hand office furniture stores) will save you money and you can find almost anything you need to get started in your business.

Once you're in business a fax machine is a real asset. You would be amazed at how much work you can do via a fax. If your computer has a built-in fax/modem, that's great . . . except there are times when you need to fax information that is not on your computer. A built-in fax/modem is not dependable either. I think technology has a long way to go before fax/modems will work properly. I have had people ask me to fax information to them and when I did they answered the phone. When I explain that I am trying to fax I get "Oh, I'm sorry. I'll turn on the fax, give me a minute". It has gotten to the point that I will not fax to someone unless they have a dedicated fax number. Personally, a separate fax, apart from your computer, is your best bet. A separate fax will serve as an interim copy machine as well. There are hundreds of different fax machines on the market. When I started out I purchased a used fax which ran for years. If your budget allows, price out a plain paper fax machine because of quality. Prices are falling. Just remember you don't want to spend a lot of money at first.

**KEEP IT SIMPLE, KEEP IT INEXPENSIVE.
AND, IF POSSIBLE . . .
GO FOR A SEPARATE FAX MACHINE.**

FILE CABINETS —
are extremely useful. You will find that the more information you receive in the mail, the more information you will want to keep. Keeping organized and having the ability to readily access any information you need will come in handy when you keep a good filing system. It also reduces stress when you know where to look for something. I have gone through the stress of not being organized, and we are all guilty of it, so I cannot stress enough the importance of being organized.

ROLODEX —
you'll be amazed at how many numbers you will acquire even if you're only working with one account in the beginning. There are numbers you will use often and there are numbers you will only use once a year or so, when you need to order supplies or books. You will also start networking via the Prodigy, CompuServe or whatever on-line service you join. There will be contacts and people you will want to stay in touch with and a Rolodex is a good place to

keep their numbers, rather than scribbling them on a piece of paper only to lose it later. I feel many of us are guilty of scribbling numbers only to be sorry later when the number is lost. Get in the habit of using a Rolodex and keep it right by your computer.

Planner —

There are many various yearly planners on the market today. I find it to be an essential tool and I always carry one. I use a Franklin Planner. It offers me the opportunity to prioritize my schedule and enables me to write a list of things to do. I write everything in my planner so there is always a record. When I'm near a phone, I always have my planner with me. Again, loose paper and stick-ems only become lost later on. If you don't want a planner in the beginning, use a notebook. The important key here is keeping everything together - even your mental notes.

It has been said that the most successful people are the most organized. Make your home office as organized and easy to maneuver around in as possible. It will make your life easier and your business will flow that much more readily.

> Organization is a good "key"
>
> to a successful business!

CHAPTER 4

THE BUSINESS PLAN

Successful small business expansions and new job formations lead the way in creating new markets, innovations and jobs. Most entrepreneurs are not adequately prepared to go into business. Although they have the desire, talent, and motivation . . . many have not taken the time to properly investigate and research the business they are interested in starting.

A business plan is very important. Many people, myself included, dive right into a business venture and don't bother with a business plan. Or they start a business and tell themselves they will write a business plan "*later*". Only later never comes.

Let's determine why people go into business:

COMMON REASONS FOR STARTING A BUSINESS:
- Being your own boss
- Financial freedom
- Not working with others

DETERMINING WHAT IS THE RIGHT BUSINESS FOR YOU:
- What do you like to do with your time?
- What skills do you have? Have you developed these skills?

- What support from family, friends, and business' will you get?
- How much time are you ready to devote to the business?
- What skills do you have that are marketable?

AND THEN
- What finances will you need?
- Can you operate your business for approximately 1 year with little or no income?
- Is your idea practical, and will it fill a need?
- What is your competition?
- What is your advantage over an existing business?
- Can you create a demand for your business?
- Will you follow a marketing plan and stay with it?

OUTLINING A BUSINESS PLAN

In any business, I cannot emphasize enough the importance of having a good business and marketing plan. In the business plan that I describe, there are marketing tips that I will discuss fully in the following chapters. There are many kinds of business plans available. Just remember "**information is power!**" Make it your business to know what business information is available, where to get it and most importantly, how to use it.

Chapter 5

Writing a Business Plan

A business plan consists of three main sections, with each section containing specific information about your company's current business and financial position. Here is a brief rundown on each element of a business plan:

I. The Introduction:

- Usually running about three pages, the first section is intended to give the reader a brief overview of the proposal.
- A title page: identifies the company and its principal officers, with name, address, and telephone numbers.
- A table of contents: listing the three principal sections and all major subheadings, and;
- A brief statement of purpose: summarizing the proposal, spelling out how much is involved, how the funds are to be used (ex: 10% marketing, 10% utilities, 50% rent, 20% for loan repayment, 10% office supplies = 100%), how the firm will benefit, and how the funds will be repaid (in the case of a loan).

II: The Description:

The comments in this section should spell out your company's current business position and its plan for the future. Be certain to address at least five areas of the following in your comments. It should also contain all the steps which will be taken to get the business started and the direction of where you would like to see the business go in 5 years. It should consist of:

•**Describe your business in as much detail as possible.** Tell what your business is, how you run it, and why you are successful.

•**Describe your market and your company's market niche.** Give some idea of your market's size and potential, and your marketing strategy. Some extra tips to include might be:

- ✔ Identifying the demand for your product/service.
- ✔ Identifying your customers and their location.
- ✔ Explaining how your product/service will be advertised.
- ✔ Discussing how your talent/service will be delivered.
- ✔ Explaining your pricing strategy and your source and amount of initial equity capital.
- ✔ Developing a monthly operating budget for year 1 and then project out 3 years of quarterly balance sheets and profit and loss statements. Provide monthly cash flow statements which tie to the quarterly balance sheets provided for a 2 year period. Discuss your break-even point and explain your personal balance sheet and method of compensation.
- ✔ Provide *"what if"* statements to demonstrate alternative approaches to addressing any negatives which may develop.

- **Describe your competition** and give some idea of how you handle it. Mince no words. If competition is severe, say so. State why your service/product is better than XYZ's and what extra advantage you are supplying that your competition is not!

- **Describe your management team,** emphasizing the business background and experience of each member of the team. Some personal data, such as age, special interests, and place of residence, should be included. Qualifications, past experiences and future education should be included. Explain the day-to-day operations of the business and discuss future needs to hire and personnel policies and procedures. Mention your lease, insurance, dues, etc. which pertain to your business.

- **Describe how the new capital will be applied.** Spell out what projects the funds will be used for. You should be as specific as possible, which means that you will have to reach some hard decisions before seeking funds.

III. The Financial Section:

Your *"financial,"* as they are commonly labeled by lenders and other providers of capital, should be aimed at providing support for the statements made in the descriptive section. You will need both historical data and projections for the future. Start off with a Source and Application of Funding statement, which shows in detail how the proceeds of the financing will be used (e.g., percentages allocated to equipment, advertising, product distribution). You can then move on to the more traditional financial statements:

•**Historical statements** should go back about 5 years. If you business is cyclical in nature, you should cover a complete cycle, even if it means digging further into the past. The reports should include balance sheets, income statements, and cash-flow statements.

•**Projections** should also include proforma balance sheets, income statements, and cash-flow statements. Summary reports are acceptable in most cases. Make sure that you include projections for at least the period that the funds will be used and repaid.

Even though you will usually need a full-blown business plan, running about 12 pages, to ensure proper treatment on most financing expeditions, there are times when a less thorough treatment will do just as well. For instance, you may already have established a close relationship with your bank and merely need to present a documented proposal to the loan committee. Or, you may be attempting to arrange new financing from a private investor who is already familiar with your company's operation. In such cases, a summary financing proposal can usually be substituted for a formal business plan.

A summary financing proposal is a "mini" business plan consisting of no more than six or seven pages. The first page contains the proposal itself, detailing the amount of cash needed, repayment schedule, collateral, and any other pertinent details.

The second page summarizes how the funds will be used and how your firm will benefit. In brief, this section sets forth your arguments on why the proposal will be a good loan or investment. This is followed by a two to three page outline on your company's history, its product and marketing position, its management team, and a summary of its prospects for the future. In short, this is a capsule version of the descriptive section of a formal business plan.

Finally, you should include a condensed balance sheet and income statement, plus a year or two of projections. Cash-flow statements would give you a substantial boost to your argument here.

Once completed, you will now have a clear direction on where you are headed. Some major corporations call this their **"Mission Statements."** Please do not be fooled into thinking this is a waste of time. This will probably be the most *valuable* thing you will ever do. My mission statement is on my brochure. I use it in my marketing and especially in my presentations.

NO TIME?

WRITE A

SHORTER PROPOSAL

Facts about a Small Business

Taxes - The IRS recommends that you attend a Small Business Tax Workshop. It will provide you with a basic introduction to business taxes.

A workshop would include:

- Tax advantages and disadvantages of sole proprietorships.
- The basics of preparing your business tax returns.
- How to withhold and make deposits of federal taxes.
- What records you need and how to keep good records.
- The functions of the IRS. This include services, tax audits, your appeal rights, and penalties a business may incur.

Also, discussing your business ideas with your personal accountant will greatly enlighten you to future advantages and future liabilities.

Chapter 6

Getting Started and Networking

Starting a business can be a trying experience and you will need to get out and meet people and become involved. I know a lot of people who are starting this business and work full-time jobs so they won't be able to be as active but by joining organizations you get free publicity and advertising.

All the organizations I will mention have newsletters, meetings and will possibly write a press release for you. You can join these organizations and they may feature you in their monthly newsletter. What better publicity could you possibly get and its free! A lot of these organizations have doctors and dentists who are members. They read newsletters too. By joining your name is listed in their roster and again, you may be the feature on a newsletters.

Networking organizations:

Better Business Bureau.
You will need to be in business for 6 months before you can join, but one of the key advantages is that you can use their name on your advertising such as "Member of the Better Business Bureau."

Chamber of Commerce -

You have all seen member of the Chamber of Commerce. A lot of doctors have their memberships posted in their office. By joining this organization you will have something in common with the medical profession and again . . . remember their newsletters.

Toastmasters -

Are you afraid of that first face to face presentation that you will make? Join Toastmasters and you will get comfortable with public speaking. They too have a newsletter and once more . . . free advertising. They meet early mornings as well for the working members.

Local Networking -

Check your local papers for professional networking luncheons. Some towns have them for woman only and others for minorities. These networking groups are there to help people get ahead in small business. Read your paper carefully and look for any groups in your area.

Chapter 7

Buzz Words —
Superbills —
Claim Forms

Before we get into marketing and pricing, I would like to make you aware of certain buzz words. In this business we all use the word "superbill." You may ask what is a superbill? A superbill is a printed piece of paper you receive from the doctor's office which lists your name and a CPT and ICD-9 code. As you read the reference section in this book you will more fully understand the difference between a CPT and ICD-9 code.

Doctors will give you a copy of their superbills and that is your guide to inputing claims into your practice management software. Remember, if you bill for a big practice, you will get about 20-30 superbills a day or possibly more. Superbills will be your record of what procedure and diagnosis the physicians office gave you and by law these have to be held for 6 years.

A claim form is a HCFA 1500 form. Somewhere in the late 1970's, the American Medical Association

(AMA) created a universal claim form that would standardize the information needed by people who are processing the completed claim forms. The claim form supplies all the information needed to file a claim and includes the patient's data such as date of birth, address, policy identification number, sex, etc. It lists the diagnostic and treatment data along with the providers identification number and the location of where the services were provided (hospital, nursing home or physicians office).

EOB - Explanation of benefits is a detailed summary of the direct payments to the health care provider, the procedures submitted on a particular claim, and the company determined fee allowed for each procedure. It will also list denials or deductables.

As you read the next chapter you will get a brief summary of books available that will help you understand the medical claims process.

Chapter 8

Reference Books

Before we begin the reference sections, let's understand why reference books give us essential information. Doctors see patients. They need to report and file to the insurance companies what the patient was seen for and why. A procedure (commonly called CPT codes) is a listing of descriptive terms and identifying codes for reporting medical services and procedures performed by a physician. It could be for a common cold. If that is the case, they would code the procedure as an Evaluation & Management. Or they could see a patient for the removal of a wart, which would then become a procedure that would be coded as a Surgical Procedure. And the list goes on and on.

Once a procedure is determined, you then need to list a diagnosis (called ICD 9-CM codes) which will tell the insurance company the reason for the procedure, service, or supply. An example of a diagnosis is whooping cough, immunity deficiency, hemorrhaging, etc.

Procedures are grouped within six major sections:

> Medicine
> Evaluation & Management (E/M)
> Anesthesiology
> Pathology & Laboratory
> Surgery
> Radiology

After the doctor codes the procedure he needs to put down a diagnosis code. The Diagnosis code is then broken into subsections according to body part, service, or diagnosis (e.g., mouth, amputation or septal defect). A diagnosis is used for indexing the specific reason, such as the classification of the disease (ex: acute conjunctivitis, unspecified osteomyelitis, or urinary tract infection). It will tell the insurance company what the reason for the visit was. The doctor uses "Evaluation & Management" commonly coded as 99212, and he discovers the patient has a urinary tract infection and his diagnosis of that code will be 599.9.

St. Anthony's, Medical Arts Press and PMIC are three excellent companies from which to purchase books. NACAP has discounts available through various vendors so check them out. When you purchase the books, read carefully and thoroughly the Preface of the books and any other pertinent information the book may have. I have purchased books from Medical Arts Press (800-826-6706) and PMIC (1-800-MED-SHOP). Both companies are excellent in their customer service departments. There are other companies out there, you may want to shop around.

Medical Arts Press is good at setting up an account immediately and billing you later. They are located in Minneapolis, Minnesota. PMIC will want a Visa or MasterCard number before sending you the books.

The two books which I feel are absolutely necessary are the ICDE 9-CM and CPT code books. Another great book is *Understanding Medical Insurance* by Joanne C. Rowell. All books can be purchased from St. Anthony's, Medical Arts Press or PMIC.

❐

The Following Books will be a Great Guide to Help you Successfully Submit Claims

ICD9-CM (listing of diagnostic codes)

You will need an ICD9-CM, Volumes 1 and 2. An ICD9-CM is the coding book used by physicians. All doctors are required by law to submit diagnosis codes for reimbursement.

ICD stands for International Classification of Diseases and therefore is known as the coding system physicians must use.

The book I use is the St. Anthony's book. It is expensive but, they supply you with updates for a full year. Coding books need to be kept current and accurate. There are changes throughout the year and you will need to update regularly. St. Anthony's will provide you with an updating service.

CPT (A listing of procedural codes)

CPT stands for Current Procedural Terminology. It is a listing of descriptive terms and identifying codes for reporting medical services and procedures performed by physicians.

The purpose of the terminology is to provide a uniform language that will describe medical, surgical, and diagnostic services accurately.

The codes serve a wide variety of important functions. It is also useful for administrative management purposes such as claims processing.

HCPCS (more specific means of coding to include modifiers)

HCPC is an acronym for **Health Care Financing Administration Common Procedure Coding System.** The pronunciation for HCPCS is "hick-picks."

This system is a uniform method for healthcare providers and medical suppliers to report professional services, procedures, and supplies. This book not only enables the operational needs of Medicare/Medicaid, it coordinates government programs by uniform application of HCFA's (Health Care Financing Administration) policies, and allows providers and suppliers to communicate their services in a consistent manner. This book is a necessary part of your library.

CDT-2 (a code book designed specifically for dental billing)

❐

Let's put HCPCs in Perspective -

Before you apply HCPC codes, check for Level III codes assigned by your local Medicare carrier, state Medicare office, or private payer.

Level I
is the CPT which lists the five digit codes with descriptive terms for reporting services performed by healthcare providers and is the country's most widely accepted coding reference.

Level II
codes are the HCPC's National Codes. CPT does not contain all the codes needed to report medical services and supplies, therefore HCFA developed the second level of codes. These codes begin with a single letter (A through V) followed by four numeric digits. They are grouped by the service or supply they represent. Unfortunately, an increasing number of private insurance carriers are also encouraging or requiring the use of HCPC's National Codes which makes this book essential in your library.

Level III
is a code assigned and maintained by individual state Medicare carriers. These codes begin with a letter, W through Z, followed by four numeric digits. These codes are not common to all carriers. These codes are used to describe new procedures that are not yet available in Level I or II. These are introduced on an as-needed basis throughout the year.

ADDITIONAL BOOKS WORTH READING ARE:

UNDERSTANDING MEDICAL INSURANCE
(by Joanne C. Rowell, published by Delmar)

I highly recommend this book, especially if you're new to this field. This is a "must." It is a step-by-step guide to understanding medical insurance. *Understanding Medical Insurance* will introduce you to different types of insurance, the complete "development" of a claim, terminology, diagnostic coding, Medicare/Medicaid, how the basic insurance claim should be filled out, BC/BS, Champus, etc. The list goes on and on. Although this book is not a must for everyone, it contains vital information that even the most experienced person might not know.

INSURANCE DIRECTORY

Although you can survive without this book, the Insurance Directory designed by Medicode, provides the most complete, accurate, and up-to-date demographic information on insurance payers across the country. You will find examples of forms for use in your office. The book provides information regarding how insurers pay claims as well as how you should submit and monitor those claims.

REIMBURSEMENT MANUAL FOR THE MEDICAL OFFICE

Guides you through each step of the reimbursement process. Covers terminology, CPT, HCPCS and ICD-9-CM, billing processes, forms, fee setting, superbill design, plus dealing with insurance carriers and managed care organizations (HMOs/PPOs).

✓ Medicare Rules & Regulations

Contains material from the official Medicare Carriers Manual.

Medical Marketing Handbook

Designed to help simplify the concepts and strategies of medical marketing. This book helps develop a comprehensive marketing plan for medical management.

Medical Acronyms, Eponyms & Abbreviations

This guide helps you translate those tricky acronyms and abbreviations. Covers all medical specialties plus nursing, administration, quality assurance, dietetics, pharmacy and lab.

Law, Liability, and Ethics for Medical Office Personnel

If you don't understand all the laws that impact a practice, this book clearly defines the statutes and regulations which affect today's medical practices.

❐

And the list goes on and on. Call PMIC or Medical Arts Press. Ask them to send you their catalog free of charge and to be put on their mailing list for specials.

HCFA forms can be purchased from almost any company. I purchased mine from Moore at 708-913-3200. At the time they were the least expensive, although that too changes daily. I believe PMIC and Medical Arts Press may carry them as well as MediSoft.

CHAPTER 9

WHAT DOCTORS WANT TO HEAR

It is a known fact that doctors are not business people. Harvard University is contemplating a mandatory course where all doctors will have to start taking some business management courses. They have their expertise in their field of study to be the very best; however, the bottom line is **they are not business minded**.

Doctors want to hear **how you can save them money** and that you have the ability to file their claims quickly and accurately so they can get their money promptly. They want to hear that you can file their claims with a 97% accuracy rate. One thing doctors **do not know** (and it will be hard to convince them), is that their office manager gives up on claims after they are rejected a few times. **Don't ever criticize their office manager for this.** You know the facts, they don't. They surely do not want you coming in and telling them their office management is not sufficient.

Unfortunately the doctor never finds out about those lost claims. In this business we call those claims the **"Mercedes or Porsche"** drawer. It would be a shame to count the thousands of dollars that are disregarded because office personnel either don't want to, or are too busy to, look for old EOB's or surgical reports to attach and refile. Or the office staff changes and the new staff doesn't file the old claims.

Whatever the reason, if you can convince the doctor, ethically, that this is happening in his practice, you may have a new client, and he can buy his new Mercedes with the money that was being disregarded. I told one doctor about the Mercedes drawer and she asked me what was that. I told her and she called me back that night and said she never thought about a Mercedes drawer but realized that was happening. So, don't put his office manager/staff down because he/she may think its the best thing that ever happened to him/her. Convince him/her that their office management is best suited to take care of his/her patients and their needs, and should not to be distracted by the mundane billing and insurance process.

If possible, try and be up on the latest news with Medicare and other health insurance companies. If you made it this far to meet with the doctor - don't mess it up . . . try networking with your peers before the meeting. Network on the on-line services (Prodigy, CompuServe, America-On-Line). Find out what procedures Medicare won't pay for before your meeting. When the doctor gives you his/her superbill you will be able to look at it and tell him/her which services are not covered. At this point, the doctor may want to code the patient differently. What you are telling him/her is not illegal! You are only telling him that a different code may apply to that patient if it were coded differently. **Don't ever tell him you can code.** Your job is not to code but to file claims. Down the road you will be able to tell the doctor that the code is obsolete now or he could use another code. But whatever you do, don't take on the task of coding. That is a tremendous responsibility for which you want no part of.

If you are able to find out if the insurance doesn't cover a particular procedure or how many visits a patient is allowed for a particular procedure you will shine in the doctor's eyes. By networking on Prodigy or any of the other on-line bulletin boards you may be able to get the information you need. You can also call your Medicare/Medicaid office in your state and find out if there is a limitation on the number of visits. If you didn't have a chance to find out the information, steer away from the subject. If something comes up that you cannot answer . . . tell him honestly, you don't know the answer, but will get back to him right away with the answer.

Since I am only familiar with MediSoft and Lytec I can only speak about the two software programs. These software programs allow you to tell the doctor how many times a patient has been seen for a particular procedure so that you can track the visits for the doctors. This is an especially good feature in tracking for Chiropractors and psychologist/psychiatrist. One word of advice, when you have your first appointment with a potential provider, discuss procedure codes for his/her specific specialty and talk about them during your visit, if possible. You will impress him/her. As I said before, networking with the on line services will help you in these areas. You could even discuss some of the difficulties of the procedures for his/her specific specialty that you picked up from the on-line services.

You should also be up on current issues, rules and regulations. The NACAP newsletter will help you in that area.

Doctors want to hear that you can make their practice function efficiently by taking the burden of billing off their shoulders. They want to know you can maximize their cash flow and that you will do everything in your power to get all claims paid.

They want to know that you're reliable and that you're capable, and above all . . . their business is your business; therefore, you plan on working hard for you.

The bottom line . . . you need to emphasize that collecting their money promptly and efficiency is a reflection on you, and therefore you will work hard for them.

ADDITIONALLY, YOU WANT THE DOCTOR TO KNOW:
- You can improve cash flow —
  in most cases by 97%.
- You are consistent —
  an average physician's employee turns over every 2.6 years. That means he/she would have to hire and train new staff which will cost him/her more money.
- Using you is Cost Effective —
  the average practice that files by paper spends between $6 - $12 a claim, you can do it electronically for $3.00 or less per claim.
- By using your billing service —
  he/she does not have to pay for vacations, sick days, or holidays. You are there and are reliable.
- Emphasize, you are an extension of his/her office - just a phone call away.

CAY Medical Management (1-603-465-6062) carries a program called **"Easy Quote"** which sells for $49.99.

It calculates customized charges for physicians. When you ask what their current cost is, many will say, "Oh, $2-$3". National statistics and the Health Care Financing Administration have come up with the cost of $8 - $10 a claim. The physicians perception and yours are quite different. By using "Easy Quote" you know that you have to show the physician that it doesn't really cost him/her $2 or $3 dollars, but $8 - $10.

With this program you will be able to key in initial costs of the secretary/data entry personnel's time in generating forms, stuffing envelopes, stamping, mailing, etc., cost of capital, cost of follow-up, billing to patients and finally overhead.

This program is worth its weight in gold and gives you a nice print out that you can leave with the doctor.

Chapter 10

Pricing your Services and Cost Projection

Pricing your services is a very tricky question. Therefore, I suggest you obtain your competitor's fees. Pricing varies throughout the country.

The fee will depend on whether you want to have a Full Service Billing Center or Claims only. Having Claims Wizard will greatly aid you in your fee structure.

Full-Service Billing Centers Include:

- Submitting claims electronically and on paper when necessary.
- Patient ledgers - which show patient activity such as charges, payments, and account adjustments. An account adjustment could be capitation because of an HMO or PPO. (Capitation is an agreement between the doctors and the HMO or PPO and refers to a set amount of money that the doctor and

insurance agree upon.) An HMO or PPO will only pay so much money for the doctors services for each individual patient whether that patient is seen by the doctor ten times or not at all. The doctors still get his/her fee by the HMO/PPO and if that patient is seen constantly it can be a loss for the doctor. By law the difference between what he/she is charging, and what an HMO/PPO pays, cannot be collected from the patient.
- Patient statements - is what you will send to the patient when you bill them for balances that are usually not covered by the insurance company.
- Management reports - are reports you give to the doctors and can include any one or all of the following:
    - Insurance analysis report
    - Capitation reports
    - An analysis of the practice which gives the doctor information on procedures, payments received and accounts.
    - An outstanding balance sheet on what is owed and what has been billed for a particular month or year.
    - Visit report - showing the doctor the number of visits allowed and the number of visits used for insurance purposes.

The fee for full-service billing varies from 5-10% of what is collected from the insurance companies. You can call around to different billing centers in your area and find out what the going rate for your area is. Although I don't suggest you do this, I do know of someone who investigated the billing centers in their area by saying they were an accountant for a doctor and was checking on billing centers to see if it were feasible for their client.

They were happy to give that individual whatever information they needed. However, the main objective here is to find out their fee and ask them to mail you an information packet. This will give you a comparison as to what your competition is.

Claims Only means:

Claims only is submitting "only claims" and is different. The average fee for a per-claim submission is anywhere from $1.50 per claim to $6.00 a claim. Again, if you call your competitor (a billing center) and find out their rate you will have a guideline to go by. This will greatly aid you in keeping your services in the competitive market. Area and location will depend on pricing your services. Billing in the Northeast could be substantially different than the Southeast. Have knowledge of your competitors fee's. It also depends on what you can actually get for your services. Also, in pricing your services, you need to know how long each claim will take you. You cannot charge $3.50 to $4.00 a claim when it only takes you one minute to do the data entry. If that were the case you would only charge $1.50 if it took you a minute to input the claim. And relatively speaking, a $1.50 a minute per claim for an hour is not bad money.

When a claim is submitted and the claim is rejected because of an office error you can charge a doctor an additional fee to resubmit the claim; however, if the mistake is yours and not the doctors, *I don't recommend charging him.* A lot may depend on your clearinghouse as well. Some clearinghouses charge an additional submission fee to resubmit a claim, while other clearinghouses tell you what the error is and the resubmission is free.

The bottom line is your fee's will be determined by what kind of specialty you are billing for and how many claims you can input in an hour. If you are billing for a physician who has a repeat business and the claims never really change much and you are entering a claim a minute, your fee would be much lower. In that case you would charge at the low end of the scale.

When you analyze the kind of business you would like to have (Full-Service vs. Claims Only) you need to consider the extra expenses of using the phone, calling insurance companies, spending money on postage, letterhead, envelopes, etc. Additionally, you need to consider your workload. You need to discuss with the physician whether or not you will be using his stationary and envelopes or supplying them yourself. That will also help you in your fee schedule. Once you can project your expenses, you will know what you need to charge.

Again, in this area a good program on the market you can buy which will help you in determining how much money to charge is ***"Easy Quote"*** from CAY Medical Management (800-221-0488). Generally speaking, most billers price out their services to about $50.00 an hour for work provided, whether it be full billing or per claim submission. The hourly fee is what you choose.

Free trials is another marketing tool many billing centers use. I don't recommend a free trial. What I do recommend is a reduced rate for 3 months to see how the working relationship is surviving and it gives you an excellent opportunity to track your time and expenses to see if you can drop your fee or will need to raise your fee. During the presentation I tell the physician/dentist that at the end of the 3 months reduced trial rate we will sit down and renegotiate the fee, and I emphasize that it could possibility be lower. I go on to say that at this time we can make changes, add services, etc. It is more of a time to make sure they are happy with the services they are receiving.

One thing people ask me over and over is "How much money can I make?" How can you tell someone how much money they can make, you can't. Let's say you are billing for a doctor that brings in over $300,000 a year and you are billing for a practice that only brings in $100,000 a year. You are charging them 7%.

It is easy to calculate that the differences in the 300,000 vs. the 100,000 @ 7% will vary.

The bottom line on billing is that you wouldn't charge a doctor $3.00 a claim if that claim takes you less than a minute to input. There are variations with every practice and with all data entry. In podiatry you could get by charging him $1.50 - $1.75 a claim whereby an internal medicine doctor you would charge $3.00 and up per claim. I found in podiatry that the patient data is repeated with a few new patients here and there. Inputting the claim is less than one minute . . . once you're familiar with the codes.

A Crash Course in Pricing Your Services:

Dr. Guido filed 200 claims a month with the average claim being $100. (*Total monthly income would be $20,000 in submitted insurance claims*). It takes you approximately 2 minutes to enter a claim. How much would you charge?

Per Claim	1.67
Flat Fee	333.50
Percent	1.7%

Let's assume you want to make $50 an hour. You would take the 200 claims and multiply that by 2 minutes and come up with 400 minutes or 6.67 hours. At $50 an hour you would multiply 6.67 by $50 and your time would be worth $333.50 a month to file 200 claims. That would be your flat fee cost. To figure out your per claim cost you would then divide the $333.50 by 200 claims and you would get $1.67 a claim. At this point figuring out your percentage is easy. All you do now is divide $20,000 by $333.50 and you come up with .016% which when rounded off comes to 1.7% equaling $340. monthly.

Dr. Dion billed out $100,000 a month and saw approximately 500 patients per months (*average bill $200*). It takes you about 4 minutes to file the claim. What would you charge?

Per claim	_____
Flat fee	_____
Percent	_____

Again, you take 500 claims x 4 minutes to come up with 2,000 minutes or 33.33 hours. At $50. an hour you multiply the $50. x 33.33 hours = $1,666.50 as a flat fee. For per claim you would divide $1666.50 by 500 to come up with $3.33 a claim. Your percentage then would be 1.66 ($100,000 divided by $1666.50). *$1666.50 by $100,000*

Now you are able to give the doctor 3 options of billing, a per claim, flat fee or percentage. When you do this the physician/dentist feels they know what they will be paying up front and down the road they won't be hit with a big bill from XYZ Billing Service. The percentage is to their advantage because you will work harder knowing that every dollar that comes in is part of your percentage.

Once again you can get "**Easy Quote**" which will do the same thing and produce a nice cost analysis for the physician/dentist. If you don't use "**Easy Quote**" you will need to take into consideration the following expenses and incorporate them in your fee.

Consider these expenses:

- Initial set-up expenses
- Office overhead/your overhead
- Advertising
- How often you pick up information

THE BOTTOM LINE :

What is your time worth?

Remember too, you can always start high and come down.

Chapter 11

Marketing Strategies

Your Key to Marketing Your Services

Marketing is the most important part of your business. Without it, you will not have any business. You need to be prepared to **budget marketing expenses and follow through faithfully** with your marketing plan. If you don't follow a marketing plan you will take your first step toward failure.

Let's assume you were planning a trip across the country. The first thing you would do is purchase a map of the states you plan on visiting, then you would mark your destination. Marketing a business is very similar. You need to know how you will get from point A to point B. You don't need too many details, just an easy plan on how you are getting there. The same thing goes for your business . . . you need to think of your goals, your projected time frame and what it will take to get there. You need to plan a budget of expenses, and you need to follow that plan. Without it you will get lost.

> A GOOD MARKETING PLAN
>
> SHOULD NOT BE FLEXIBLE.

Different types of marketing are radio, newspaper, magazines, television, direct mail, cold calling, yellow pages, brochures, telephone marketing, trade shows, public relations, press release, and most importantly, word of mouth and referrals.

The most common type, although not the most effective, is direct mail since most people hate the "cold-call approach." You can obtain a book of computerized information which will include doctors by states and their individual specialty. Or you can order a listing of doctors in your area who are not filing electronically from CAY Medical Management (1-800-221-0488) or possibly from your local Medicare Carrier. This will enable you to narrow in on one specialty or assess every doctor. You need to market these doctors a minimum of 3 times to get your name out.

Decide your strategy, draw your road map on how you would like to get there, and follow it through faithfully. Don't quit after a month or two. If you decide you want to take another route in marketing, finish out your original plan first before you decide to switch direction. You need to be consistent.

Chapter 12

Cold Calling

Cold calling is the most effective means of marketing. If you are cold calling remember the old rule is for every 20 no's you will get one yes. In this business it may be for every 50 no's, you will get a yes. You are selling a service, and eventually you will find a person who is in need of that service. Take packets with you the day you cold call and if you get a foot in the door . . . **leave a packet if the interest is there.** Otherwise, take brochures with you and leave them with the receptionist. If you can get the name of the office manager, leave the brochure and call her back in a few days. Make sure on the day you cold call you look your best. It is proven that you need to dress for success.

Cold calling is the most effective way to getting an appointment and without a doubt, it is the least expensive way of marketing. I think cold calling is the hardest of all marketing for a person to do. Everyone has different feelings about it. You may know a sales person who has been trained to do this, if so . . . . get some tips.

The five steps to cold calling are:

- Getting the attention of the person
- Identifying yourself and your company
- The reason for the call
- A qualifying or questioning statement
- Setting the appointment

Did you know it is easier for doctors to use your service if they take the first step of requesting more data? Try offering the doctor/office manager your brochure and an opportunity to come back for a "free consultation." This offer may get you an appointment. At the appointment, which is the actual meeting, you are on a personal basis and it is the time to then sell yourself and your service. There are also some words that we call ***"buzz"*** words. Use them in your vocabulary and brochures.

These words will carry a lot of weight. Use them often. They are:

Free	*New*	*Introducing*
Save	*Discover*	*Results*
Easy	*Proven*	*Guaranteed*
Benefits	*Alternative*	*Trustworthy*
Comfortable	*Proud*	*Safe*
Security	*Winnings*	*Value*
Advice	*Announcing*	*Why*
Your	*People*	*Money*

Words which could be intimidating. Try not to use:

Buy	*Obligation*	*Failure*
Bad	*Sell*	*Loss*
Difficult	*Wrong*	*Decision*
Deal	*Liability*	*Hard*
Contract	*Fail*	*Cost*
Worry		

CHAPTER 13

NEWSPAPERS
FOLLOWING THE HELP WANTED ADS

You can either place an ad about your service in the local newspaper or you can follow the classifieds. Every time you see someone advertising for a medical biller, send them your brochure and a cover letter. The following is an example of an appropriate cover letter on your stationary.

NOTE: If you follow through with the Sunday papers every week, and find billing ads, then send them your cover letter and brochure. I know someone who was very successful using this technique. All of their doctors were landed this way.

> Life is like a fine painting,
> we must choose each
> color well and
> cherish each stroke

Dear Provider:

I would like to introduce myself and my billing service. I am an independent billing center which files insurance claims electronically. My experience includes years of medical billing & claims processing as well as hospital administration. I am certified by the National Electronic Billers Association. To keep up on the latest changes in the healthcare industry I attend conferences and stay aware of the continuous changes in the health care industry.

When you read through the enclosed material, you will understand that it is far more advantageous for you to use our services to file your Medicaid/Medicare and commercial claims than it is to file them in-house.

If you were paying an employee $8 an hour based on a 20 hour week, you have already spent $160.00 in salary for a week, or $8,320 a year. In addition you are also paying for vacation, sick days, holidays, and benefits, etc. Let your office staff put their time towards extraordinary patient care, their health and follow-up phone calls and let XYZ Billing Service submit your claims. We do not call in sick, take vacation days, and spend your money making personal calls. Your success is our number one priority, and getting your money back quickly and into your own bank account is our goal.

I would welcome the opportunity to sit and meet with you and give you a cost comparison. You will see how much you can save. I will also show you how we can submit your claims fast and in the most expedient way. Feel free to contact me at your convenience.

Sincerely,

Sally Dodge
President

Another example of a cover letter you could send from responding to the "help wanted ads" might read something like . . .

Dear Dr. Heart:

Statistics show that even if your staff is consistent with resubmissions of insurance claims the time it takes you to receive insurance payments can take months and sometimes even years. This means that your cash flow is seeping away whereby if you utilized the benefits of XYZ, you could be collecting interest on your money. Filing claims manually result in account errors. However, when claims are filed electronically they have a 97% accuracy rate and are made payable before they are submitted. XYZ can reduce the time it takes for you to be paid from 17-28 days.

XYZ can file claims for private insurance carriers as well as Medicare and Medicaid. You may be presently filing Medicare claims on a computer and then printing the claims out on a HCFA form to mail. This is not filing claims electronically. It is manual paper submission. You can build your practice by letting XYZ file all your insurance claims and the reimbursement will be prompt. Electronic claims are processed ahead of paper claims!

We're experienced, confident and dedicated to providing your practice with an electronic claims processing system. If your staff spends a lot of time and money rectifying the insurance claims nightmare, XYZ is the solution. Electronic claims processing will be mandatory in the near future. Now is the time to get on-line for the future.

Should you have any questions or wish to discuss electronic billing, I will contact your office to schedule an appointment and we can discuss our state-of-the-art claims processing system.

Sincerely,

Chapter 14

Direct Marketing:
Press Releases —
Hospitals—
Advertising—

Press Releases

Have you ever wondered about your daily newspaper and the "Who's Who in Business" section? Look for it. See what they say. There is no reason why you cannot write a press release about your business and send it to the newspapers in your area/state.

> "Mrs. Sally Dodge of XYZ Billing Service has opened a Medical Billing service in the area".

Then you proceed to tell something about yourself that would be an asset. Even if you have been in business, write a press release anyway

> "Mrs. Sally Dodge is expanding her services to include electronic dental submission".

I'm sure when you look at the press releases in your newspapers you can write an essay on yourself. If you have no prior experience in the field, go on to say

Mrs. Dodge is the parent of three, a little league coach, etc. She is a member of the National Electronic Billers Association.

I think by now you understand what I am saying. The best part is that a press release is free advertising. What better way is there to get the word out?

Hospitals

Call or write the hospitals in your area, ask them if you can set up a table to be available for doctors and/or office managers to discuss the future of, and advantages, of electronic claims submission. Give them a "free cost analysis" which you can do with Easy Quote. Have brochures available and a spreadsheet of savings. Once you establish a date, put flyers in the mailbox of the doctors or send out flyers to the area physicians telling them you will be on hand that date. You might even want to include the date in a press release.

If you know someone that works in a hospital you might try having them leave your brochures in the doctors lounge. Usually the doctor will be in the lounge in between surgery or going over paperwork with a cup of coffee. If your brochure is appealing, they will pick it up.

Advertising

Call you local AMA. See if you can advertise in their monthly newsletter. There is a fee, but your name will be advertised. Hopefully you will get a call. The advertisement can be simple - "97% return on your money, the money goes directly to you, our fees are competitive. Call for a free consultation." With a little imagination you can write a great ad, but remember to

keep it simple. Give them enough information to stir their curiosity to make the call, but not too much information where there is no need to call you. I strictly do all my marketing in the AMA Newsletter. They call me, I don't call them. It also doesn't put them on the defensive, they are calling you! You have something they may be interested in.

YELLOW PAGES— List your business phone as a business line and you get a free listing in the yellow pages of your local phone book. Not only is the free listing important, but you will be listed in the information directory. You never know if your number was misplaced but they remembered your company name. They can at least call information and get your companies phone number.

DIRECT MARKETING

Direct marketing is the easiest way to market. You can mail postcards, letters and brochures. If by now you have decided cold calling is not for you, then the most successful marketing plan I have seen is the postcard approach or the direct brochure/letter mailing. The postcard approach statistics are relatively good. The doctor's office will take the two minutes to fill out the card and mail it back to you. Don't forget to provide a stamped card for return to your address.

The letter/brochure approach is also a good approach, because the brochure will have statistics and information about your service and a letter you enclose will explain your services. If the doctor is in the position at that time to use a billing service, you may have it made. If not, don't get discouraged. In 2-3 months send back another type of marketing literature to the same practice. If you decide to use the phone book, I suggest you don't send to a group of doctors in one practice. You are wasting your money because one letter to the practice/office manager should be sufficient. I prefer to market the doctors with small practices and specialties (the chiropractors, podiatrists, psychiatrists/psychologists, and ambulance companies) while others prefer to market the big practices. You have to test the market in your area. You can also call your phone company and get a phone book for every town/city in your state. Most of the phone companies will supply it free of charge.

Remember, with mail-outs, the mail never gets through to the person that they are addressed to. If you use the mail, follow-up. Send 25-100 postcards or letters and brochures a week, depending on your budget and your allowable time to follow-up on the marketing material you mailed out. Follow-up is the key to marketing. If you are sending out a survey letter or postcard with a return, statistics show that the return is less than 2%. However, in my experience with the post-card/survey letter approach, the return is 6-8% while others see a 2-3% return. Again, I cannot reiterate enough . . . this business will take time, perseverance and patience. If your return is 0%, don't get defeated.

"YOU CAN'T LEARN TO WIN
UNTIL YOU LEARN TO LOOSE"

REMEMBER FOR EVERY 20 NO'S
YOU WILL FINALLY GET A YES.

Chapter 15

Postcards
&
Brochures

Pages 72 & 73 show a sample of the postcard approach. The postcards should be perforated for easy tearing. The doctors office will read the postcard, and hopefully answer quickly. The one thing about sending postcards out is you need to **pre-stamp the return** for their convenience. It gets extremely costly, so limit yourself to 25-100 a week (depending on your budget and marketing plan).

> Many people who have used the postcard approach have found the return to be 5-8% which is high for a mailing.

Study the postcard carefully. Did you notice there isn't anything on the postcard indicating which doctors office is filling out the survey card and mailing it back to you? The reason for that is simple. They are more likely to fill out the postcard and answer the questions when they think it is just a survey and not a billing center. So that is why you have to code each and every postcard with a number in small print in the corner of the return postcard. You will also need a book with the codes so when the postcards come back and has a #1 on it, you can look in the book and see who doctor #1 was. (Ex: Dr. Smith will be #1 in the book and #1 on the postcard, Dr. Jim will be #2 in the book and #2 on the postcard and so on.) This is very important in sending out postcards.

On the other hand, you may want to have their name and address on the card. It is a matter of personal preference. They may fill it out knowing that you will have your name for the survey. The decision between having their name on the card or not is your choice.

The postcard approach has been very successful. Another tip on postcard mailings is to have the cards professionally printed which will cost about $80 per 1,000. I have found that the success of the postcard has been with people who have used this approach and spent the extra dollars in having the postcards printed on a pale linen paper (light blue or pink rather than plain white).

Study the postcard on pages 72 &73. You may need to make a copy of the postcard and glue it together (front and back). This will aid you more in knowing how it will look. Get out paper and experiment how you would like your postcard to look. Fold it several times to make sure the wording is correct and not upside down. There is still one side that has no wording. Be creative and put something inspiring there or a logo, or better yet a "fact" about your billing service or your mission statement.

But remember to get it right. My first postcard was a disaster. I had it printed all wrong and it was my own fault for not laying it out properly. I knew what I wanted and thought the printer knew what I wanted, only to find out later that the postcards were wrong. I had to separate every card to make it right. Unfortunately, sometimes we have to talk to printers like we are talking to a child. Once you take it to the printers and they print it the way you said, you've spent your money. ***If it doesn't fold right . . . it's your mistake and your money.***

```
┌─────────────────────────────────────┐
│         ┌─────────────────┐         │
│         │  Sample postcard │         │
│         │      Side A     │         │
│         └─────────────────┘         │
│                                     │
│                                     │
│                 Address             │
│                 Doctors             │
│                                     │
│                                     │
│   ┌─────────┐      ┌──────────────┐ │
│   │  here   │      │   here       │ │
│   │  stamp  │      │  goes here   │ │
│   │  your   │      │billing address│ │
│   │  place  │      │  Your full   │ │
│   └─────────┘      └──────────────┘ │
│                                     │
│     fold with easy perforation goes here │
│ - - - - - - - - - - - - - - - - - - │
```

We would greatly appreciate you taking the time to answer and return this stamped postcard of questions pertaining to medical insurance claims processing:

                                        Yes   No

Do you process medical forms for your patients? _____

Do you use computerized means to directly _____
process and send medical insurance
forms to carriers (Medicare, Medicaid,
Private Carriers)?

Do you contract with someone to _____
process your claims?

Are your accounts receivables over 30 days? _____

Would you like to recieve information _____
on available claims processing
systems/services?

```
┌─────────────────────────────────────────┐
│        ┌───────────────────┐            │
│        │  Sample postcard  │            │
│        │      Side B       │            │
│        └───────────────────┘            │
│                                         │
│                                         │
│   Doctors address is on the flip side of this
│   portion                               │
│                                         │
│   Since this side is blank you may want to
│   use your company's mission statement or
│   any motivational phrase.              │
│                                         │
│                                         │
│                                         │
├─────────────────────────────────────────┤
│                                         │
│  Questionaire is on the  ┌──────────┐   │
│  flip side               │  Place   │   │
│                          │  Stamp   │   │
│                          │  Here    │   │
│                          └──────────┘   │
│                                         │
│         ┌─────────────────────┐         │
│         │     Your Full       │         │
│         │  Mailing Address    │         │
│         │                     │         │
│         └─────────────────────┘         │
│                                         │
└─────────────────────────────────────────┘
```

Brochure/Letter Approach

There are many other ways of getting your foot in the doctor's office. I know quite a few people who have sent out brochures with a cover letter and were quite successful. You can create your own brochure with minimum skill using a computer. There are all sorts of helpful aids, including an inexpensive Color Bubble Jet Printer for colorful marketing. Paper Direct has a large array of paper products to aid you in your advertising. They also have a template to help you. I suggest calling and asking them to send you their catalog. You can also get a free packet of samples of their stationary. It is minimal in cost and well worth making the phone call to Paper Direct. Their number is 1-800-A-PAPERS.

You can save money by making your own brochures which can look just as professional as if you were to have a printer do them. You need to adjust and modify a brochure fully until you feel comfortable with sending it out. You may decide to use one of the sample letters in this booklet to send with your brochure. Try sending a brochure with or without the letter. You need to test your market and remember you will have to mail again to these doctors in three months anyway.

Did you know you can buy many different kinds of brochures from Paper Direct? You can then customize your own brochures on your own computer and print them yourself. They also have matching stationary and Rolodex cards which are perforated to go along with your brochure.

Paper Direct's unique design printed paper is the easiest and the least expensive way to add the impact of color to your brochures and stationary. You can save time and money by using your own printer to produce professional, colorful brochures. You have the flexibility to print as few or as many as you need. They also offer a complete presentation set for $99.95 which includes 100 laser postcards, 100 laser business cards, 75 brochure/mailers, 100 letterhead and envelopes, 100 paper frames, 10 presentation folders and envelopes and 12 designer laser labels. If you don't need the presentation package, they have an array of individually priced paper products. Check them out, it's well worth your time.

Sending out a brochure with a survey letter is also a good means of marketing. Don't make your marketing materials in a hurry. Spend time on them, look at them, examine for errors, and lastly, sleep on it. The next day review what you have created and see if you can improve it. Make sure your letter and brochure is in superb condition. Don't forget, as with cold calling this brochure may lead you to an appointment.

(brochure sample on pages 76 & 77)

> ***Remember —***
> Design your own brochure.
> I'm offering samples only.
> I'm sure you have a lot of
> good ideas you'll want to
> incorporate into a brochure.
> Get other people's brochures and
> compare, change, and add.
> Once you have your brochure how
> you want it, it will look great!

76 MEDICAL BILLING: THE BOTTOM LINE

XYZ BILLING SERVICE

ARE YOU CONCERNED ABOUT YOUR CLAIMS?

With consistent claims submission and the use of ECS, **DOCTORS SEE THEIR MONEY FAST,** often within **TWO WEEKS.**

XYZ'S OBJECTIVE...

XYZ works hard to maintain a close working relationship with every doctor's office.

We encourage open communication between our billing staff and the physician's office.

By treating our office as an extension of each practice, there is less chance of billing errors or patient problems.

◇

NO OBLIGATION

Yes, I'm interested in obtaining more information on electronic claims submission.

Please complete this questionnaire and mail or fax to XYZ. Filling out this questionnaire does not in anyway obligate you to use our services.

> Follow up is the key to **STEADY CASH FLOW.** XYZ's intense follow-up procedure are simply unmatched!

My practice currently has ___ employees.
We see approximately ___ patients each month.
We process approximately ___ claims each month.
Our average dollar value per claim is: ___
Do you use a computer to file claims? ___
What % of your claims are returned unpaid due to errors or omissions? ___

Name: _____
Phone #: _____

ABOUT OUR FEES

FEES...

XYZ works on a percentage or per claim basis. There are no hidden costs. you are only billed for what you collect.

OUR FEES INCLUDE...

—Postage
—Electronic Claims Submission (ECS)
—Statements/Envelopes
—Claim Forms
—Collection Action
—Management Reports

◇

| PROFESSIONALS
FOR
PROFESSIONALS |

Why Use XYZ?

Treating your patients effectively is only *half* the challenge of a successful Medical Practice . . . running it as an efficient business is the other half.

XYZ, a member of NEBA is a full-service medical billing office utilizing the latest claim processing techniques.

XYZ maintains and updates their knowledge of carrier regulations by attending numerous classes and seminars so that your claims keep up with today's changes.

XYZ will help you avoid unneeded expenditures on costly software upgrades.

XYZ will eliminate the need to hire additional staff or train new staff. You can eliminate the cost of paying for vacations, sick pay, or workers compensation.

XYZ will follow-up on delinquent claims; claims which help you eliminate the expense of a collection agency.

◆

Mailing Address

XYZ Billing
1000 Super Highway
USA 00001-1000

XYZ
Insurance
Filing Service, Inc

◆

XYZ Billing Service
1000 Super Highway
Speed Way, USA 00001-1000
800-001-0001
Fax 800-002-0002

CHAPTER 16

LETTERS
&
MARKETING TECHNIQUES

Mailing out letters can be beneficial when you enclose a brochure. But then again, it may not be beneficial. It is almost impossible to determine which is better . . . postcard or a letter.

This is a true story. A flyer was sent out at Christmas time to about 700 doctors. Not one response was received which was quite discouraging. About eight months later I received a call from a physical therapist office who was interested in outsourcing their commercial claims and wanted information. Needless to say, although we get discouraged when we don't get a response, many doctors/office managers file away information for later use or "just in case."

That is why I tell you this business will not get you rich overnight. It takes time, and sometimes it takes a lot of time. My words of advice is be patient, be persistent and eventually you will be successful.

The following are various samples of marketing letters. Design your own, you may want to add to them. I enclose a brochure with my letters when I send them out. I never received a response from the letters, but a friend of mine in California landed four doctors that way.

ONE WORD ABOUT OFFERING FREE OFFERS:

A free offer to file claims for two weeks, 30 days, etc. is something you offer the perspective physician to show them the advantages of electronic claim submission and hopefully you will be able to sign them up.

However, two weeks time is not sufficient for them to see the fast return on their money UNLESS you sign up with a clearinghouse, or go Medicare direct. If you sign up with a clearinghouse, it will take you at least 2-3 weeks to process your paperwork and get approval. Once that is in place, you can offer this free trial.

Therefore, the **bottom line** on filing free claims is once a doctor agrees to try your trial, you need to let him know that it will take 2-3 weeks for you to sign on with the Clearinghouse before you can submit his claims on a trial basis. Once that is approved you are ready to start his/her free trial.

Dear Provider:

XYZ Billing Service is privately owned and we have expanded in your area. My company is comprised of more than ten years of hospital/office administration experience, medical billing, and claims processing.

A successful medical practice provides for patients effectively! Equally important is running your practice as an efficient business. That is why XYZ can help you. XYZ Billing Service will allow your staff to do what they do best by reducing their workload and increasing your cash flow.

Electronic Data Interchange (EDI) has revolutionized the travel and banking industries. Now EDI is revolutionizing the medical industry. Inaccurate insurance filing will be eliminated at a savings far less than you yourself can do it and there will be no more overlooked claims!

>You Can Save Money . . .
>And Make More Money,
>At No Additional Cost

I would very much like to meet with you, or your office administrator, and explain how I can provide these services. At the same time I will be able to explain how the insurance companies are getting interest on your money when you should be collecting the interest.

I appreciate the time you took to read this and look forward to hearing from you. If you have any additional questions or need further information, please do not hesitate to contact me.

Sincerely,

Sally Dodge

Or You Could Try a Survey Letter Like This:

**XYZ BILLING SERVICE
100 MAIN STREET
ANYTOWN, USA 00000**

Sally Dodge
President

Telephone 000-000-000
Fax 000-000-000

Dear Provider:

I would like to offer electronic claims processing in the area and have taken the liberty of asking you to participate in this survey. I would appreciate a few minutes of your time by asking you to fill this out and return it to us in the enclosed self-addressed stamped envelope.

1. How many medical insurance claims does your practice process on a weekly basis?

    ( ) Less than 50   ( ) 50-75   ( ) 75-100   ( )100+

2. In your estimation, how much do you think processing EACH medical claim cost you?

    ( ) $3 - $4   ( ) $5 - $6   ( ) $7 - $8   ( ) unknown

3. What is the length of time it takes you to receive payment from the insurance company?

    ( )Less than 1 month ( ) 1-3 months ( ) 3-6 months

4. Have you investigated electronic claims processing?

   ( ) Yes   ( ) No

5. Do you currently process any claims electronically?

   ( ) Yes   ( ) No

6. If electronic processing were offered to you, and it cut down considerably on your wait time and total expenses to process medical claim forms, would you consider using it?

   ( ) Yes   ( ) No

Thank you for taking the time to answer our survey. Should you desire additional information by mail on the Electronic Claims Processing System that we will soon be offering in your area, please provide a contact name and a phone number. If you do not wish to receive information at this time, you may leave the area blank.

Doctor Name: _____

Contact Name: _____

Phone #: _____

Address: _____

HERE IS GOOD EXAMPLE OF A MEETING CONFIRMATION LETTER. IF ALSO SERVES AS A REMINDER OF YOUR MEETING.

Dear Dr. Right:

Thank you for agreeing to meet with me on (day & date) at (time).

In order to prepare for our meeting, please fill out the following information and mail or fax back to me at your earliest convenience. This questionnaire is designed to determine if electronic claims submission would be appropriate for your office if it would be cost-effective for you to use a billing service. You are in no way obligated to use our services by filling out this form.

1. How many employees work full-time in the office tending to phones, billing, etc.?

2. How many employees work part-time in the office?

3. Approximately how many patients do you see each month?

4. Approximately how many medical insurance claim forms do you process weekly?

5. How much time do you feel in consumed processing medical claims?

6. How much is the average claim?

7. What do you feel your time span is on receiving payment from insurance companies?

8. Do you feel some of your claims are uncollectable? If so, what percentage?

Any additional information you feel I need before our meeting, please list here:
_____
_____
_____

Thank you for taking the time to send this form back to me. I look forward to meeting you.

Sincerely,
Sally Dodge
XYZ Billing Service

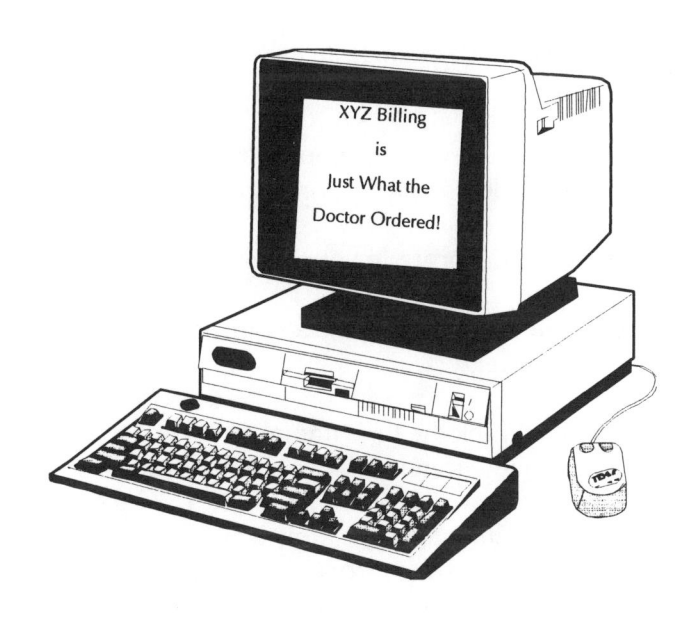

Here is a Great Survey Letter to be Mailed out with a Brochure

Dear Provider:

XYZ Billing Center is sending this questionnaire to all area physicians to find out if there is a need for claims to be filed electronically. If you can, please take a moment and answer the following questions. All answers will be kept confidential. This does not, in any way, obligate you to use our services.

1. Does your practice use a computer?

2. Do you process insurance claims for your patients?

3. Are your insurance claims electronically submitted?

4. How many people do you employ (this does not include any professional staff)?

5. How many patients are in your care?

6. What is your estimation of the amount of claims filed weekly?

7. What do you think the time frame is in receiving money from insurance companies?

8. What is your estimation of claims which are returned because of errors/omissions?

9. What percentage of your practice do you consider are bad debt?

Any other information you would like to share, please write here:

_____
_____
_____
_____
_____
_____
_____

Practice Name: _____

Phone # (optional): _____

Practice Address: _____

Thank you for your time.

Sincerely,

Sally Dodge
President
YXZ Billing Service

Sample Direct Mail Letter

Dear Physician:

I would like to introduce you to XYZ Billing Service. Our specialty is submitting claims electronically directly to the clearinghouse. By doing this, claims are immediately edited for errors and forwarded to the over 2,500 insurance carriers across the country. We do this using MediSoft, the most advanced, up-to-date specialized software. Using our service will help your staff to have a reduced workload, end the agonizing task of filing medical insurance claims, and allow them more time to follow-up on your patients. The result is a higher cash flow in your pocket.

If you were to use our service you would:

- see improved cash flow (direct payment in 18-21 days directly to you)
- know that your claims are being submitted overnight with a confirmation of claim acceptance
- see reduced paperwork
- lower your overhead

XYZ is confident that you will like processing your claims electronically. We are offering a 30 DAY FREE TRIAL OFFER! You can receive an entire month's worth of electronic claims submission on us. If at the end of 30 days, if you are not satisfied, you will be under NO OBLIGATION to continue.

Call us today for a free consultation or to start your free trial. You'll be glad you did.

Sincerely,

> **NOTE**: You may want to limit the amount of free claims you are offering.

Dear Dr. Guido:

Electronic claims processing is the future. As you're aware, Medicare has been trying to make filing of claims mandatory. XYZ Billing Service can help you file your claims and, at the same time, improve your cash flow. We can give you overnight confirmation on your claims being submitted, reduce your error rate, lower your overhead, reduce paperwork, and have your checks sent DIRECTLY to you.

For a limited time only, we are offering -

AN INTRODUCTORY FREE TRIAL.

We will submit your *Medicare/Medicaid claims free for 60 days at absolutely no cost to you. You will be under no obligation to continue if you are not absolutely satisfied.

I would like to stop by and give you a written cost comparison. You will be under no obligation. Please call me today and we can schedule an appointment.

Sincerely,

Sally Dodge

* Offer limited to 25 Medicare/Medicaid claims a day. Subject to acceptance by Medicare and does not include any resubmission because of office error. Offer expires on _____.

Dear Dr. Casey:

XYZ Billing Center has expanded in your area. If you are submitting claims manually, we can help you. All claim submitted electronically are paid faster (usually within 18-21 days) as compared to a paper claim which has a floor time of 28 days.

We are committed to helping physicians get their money quickly. Right now the insurance companies are getting interest on your money! Shouldn't you be getting that interest? XYZ can provide you with:

- Improved cash flow (the money goes directly to you and payment is made in 18-21 days)
- Confirmation of your accepted/rejected claims
- Reduced error rate
- Reduced paperwork
- Lower your overhead

XYZ would like to give you a "free cost analysis" and discuss the advantageous of electronic claims submission. Please contact us at your earliest convenience, and we would be happy to discuss the benefits of filing claims electronically.

Sincerely,

Sally Dodge
XYZ Billing Service

Dr. Poor Cashflow
777 Money Green Street
Poor Bank Account, Money Bloom, USA

Dear Dr. Poor Cashflow:

30-40% of all insurance claims filed contain errors. XYZ Billing Center can help cut through the red tape and file your claims with a 97% accuracy rate. You will see your claims paid in 18-21 days.
We submit claims directly to the clearinghouse where they are edited and sent to over 2,500 insurance carriers nationwide. The clearinghouse also notifies us of any errors or omissions. This means we can correct the claim and send it right back for resubmission.

XYZ has state-of-the-art computers and software to remove the headaches of filing insurance claims. We are able to give you management reports, insurance analysis reports, and a patient receivable ledger report which will help greatly in your cash flow.

Please call XYZ for a "free cost analysis" and let us explain how we can save you time and money. Our fees are competitive, and we will work hard to see that you get interest on your money. Why should the insurance company collect the interest?

We are available at your convenience to discuss our services. I look forward to hearing from you.

Sincerely,

Sally Dodge
XYZ Billing Center

FREE . . .
ELECTRONIC CLAIMS SUBMISSION FOR TWO WEEKS!

Dear Dr. Tri:

Let XYZ submit your claims electronically for two full weeks. Did you know medical claims processing service will reduce paperwork, errors, and tremendously improve your cash flow? Right now the insurance companies are getting interest on your money . . . why shouldn't you get that interest? XYZ is offering a free trial to allow you the opportunity of benefiting from the advantages of our services.

Your staff can now have the time to follow up on patients rather than have the headache of filing claims for your patients. We are trained experts in the field of electronic claims submission and when it comes to claims you will see a marked difference.

We will process your claims within 24 hours directly to a clearinghouse and you will be able to see a reduced rejection rate. Our clearinghouse directly sends your claims to over 2,500 carriers nationwide.

This RISK-FREE, NO OBLIGATION OPPORTUNITY will allow you the opportunity to benefit from the state-of-the-art electronic claims submission process. If, at the end of the two weeks, you are not completely satisfied, you owe us nothing. If you are happy with what you see, we will show you how inexpensive it is to have us file your claims electronically.

Either way, THIS IS A NO RISK OFFER, which expires on _____. We look forward to speaking with you.

Sincerely,

_____

NOTE: You need to get on-line with a Clearinghouse before this trial offer can begin or let the physician know that it will take 3 weeks before the trail offer can begin.

Chapter 17

Packets and What to Include

Sending a Packet in the Mail

The simplest and most inexpensive way to get a packet together for your prospective doctor is to type it on your computer, have it copied at the local office supply store and buy folders that have pockets on both sides. You can probably get 6 for a dollar. They also have a slit for your business card to be inserted.

You can put the following information on one side as well as a brochure from NEIC and your brochures and additional information on the other side.

The NEIC brochure (#59450.0PG) is a colorful brochure which lists some of the larger insurance companies who accept electronic claims. Their number is 1-800-877-0004.

My Packets Contain:

- An introduction letter (which will be your first page)

- A brief summary of the company

- Statistics (statistics speak louder than words)

- Cost analysis of filing paper vs. electronic

- A recent announcement as to Medicare rules or which electronic claims will be mandatory.

- Any news articles I feel might be of interest

On the following pages, I have given you an example of various pages I might include in the packet.

I only send packets out when I receive a postcard back from the provider requesting information, or a lead from cold calling. Possibly you may send a packet out to a provider who is need of your services.

You may also want to spend extra money and send a packet when you follow the help wanted ads in the newspapers. I have a friend in Chicago who does it this way and in one week alone, she received four replies and landed one account. This method is certainly an extra expense, however, it did work for her. Keep a list of all packets you send out, as well as postcards received. You will need to follow-up on each and every prospective physician. Call them in a few days. Ask them if they received your packet and if they have any questions. Ask them if you could come in and discuss the materials with them personally.

To gather your materials you may decide to use or modify some of the example letters or brochures described in this manual. I also suggest reviewing your competitors materials. It will aid you in developing your own unique marketing packet.

I never give a price quote in a packet. You really cannot quote them a fee until you know how many claims they submit, and how long it will take you.

When sending a packet I use a two-sided folder where my business card can be inserted. I usually put a cover letter and information about my business on one side and on the other side I put information about the clearinghouse and some statistics. You may even have some newspaper articles that you copied about electronic claims submission that you can insert. Then I'll include some statistical data, similar to the following examples, and make a little booklet (like a report) which I enclose in my packet.

BUSINESS IS LIKE AN

AUTOMOBILE

IT WON'T RUN ITSELF,

EXCEPT DOWNHILL

An Introduction Letter

Dear Dr. Poor:

Thank you for expressing an interest in XYZ Billing Service. I have enclosed some information for your review. We are medical billing experts in the Northeast, specializing in electronic claims processing which goes directly to the Clearinghouse. We can:

- submit your claims with a turnaround of 3-14 days - payment in 17-28 days,
- cut your rejection rate by 33% and,
- lower your billing costs

Your patients will see how efficient their bills are being handled. They will also be able to reach us at any time to discuss their insurance processing needs.

XYZ can greatly reduce your error rate and improve your collection rate with a drastic reduction in the actual cost of processing. It is currently costing you an average of $8 to $12 to file a claim per AMA statistics.

The enclosed information will introduce you to XYZ. We are up on the latest changes relating to the future formats in which a provider will be able to submit claims.

Beginning July 1, 1996, HCFA has mandated that Medicare can no longer accept claims received in "local formats." The new formats for claims submission are the ANSI 837 and new National Standard Format (NFS). All others will be discontinued.

Let XYZ take the hassle out of billing. Call 800-123-4567. We will provide you with the personal attention you deserve.

Sincerely

XYZ Billing Service

Electronic Filing and Practice Management

THE

PRESCRIPTION

TO MANAGING

HEALTH CARE

PRACTICES

OF THE 90'S

100 Main Street
Anytown, USA 03030
800-000-0000
Fax:800-000-0000

> A fact sheet about your company
> and the services you provide would
> be similar to the following:

XYZ

Billing Service

XYZ is a full-service billing center that recently began an aggressive marketing effort due to the recognition by physicians for a need to file claims electronically. The end result is a positive impact on medical practices.

Health care has become the largest industry in the United States. The growing senior citizen population is one reason that spending on healthcare is now over approximately $700 billion, and has grown over the last year at an exceedingly high rate.

Submitting claims directly to a Clearinghouse represents a revolutionary advance within the health care and insurance industries.

For both insurers and providers, an excellent opportunity for achieving the goals of better services, cost efficiency, and increasing productivity is modernizing the time consuming task of manually processing paper insurance claims.

XYZ is a full-service billing and insurance claim filing service offering efficient billing to both doctors and patients. With consistent claims submission and the use of electronic claims submission, doctors see their money fast, *often within two weeks.* Follow-up is the key to steady cash flow and XYZ's intense follow-up procedures is simply unmatched.

Our success depends on your success; therefore, XYZ works hard to maintain a close working relationship with every doctor's office. We encourage open communication between our billing staff and the physician's office. By treating our office as an extension of each practice, there is less chance of billing errors or patient problems.

Our fees are customized and based on a percentage or fee per claim basis. There are no hidden costs. The money goes directly to you using your EOBs. We bill you only for what you collect. Our fee's include. . . postage, electronic claims submission, statements and envelopes, claims forms, collection action, management reports, monthly billing to patients, personalized handling of all patient inquires relating to their bills, follow-up with insurance carriers, and an 800 number for your patients to call us.

Our goal is to help you obtain your money as quickly as possible. We are current in federal and state regulations and attend on-going education and seminars relating to the health care industry. XYZ is dedicated to providing your practice with an efficient, cost effective service that can improve your cash flow and build a good patient relationship.

XYZ BILLING SERVICE

PROVIDING...

~ *Electronic filing of claims and paper filing when required*

~ *Patient, secondary & tertiary billing*

~ *Weekly reporting showing all claims submitted*

~ *Follow-up on claims submitted for payment*

~ *Eligibility and benefit verification*

~ *Reconciliation of delinquent accounts receivable*

~ *Patient insurance aging reports and practice analysis reports are available monthly, semi-annually and annually*

XYZ Will Give You. . .

Submitted Daily Summary - this report informs the provider of how many claims were accepted and rejected by files submitted.

Provider Daily Statistics - this report contains statistics by batch for each provider. Rejected batches and claims are listed with detailed error explanations. It is imperative that this report be reviewed after each transmission to prevent "lost" claims.

Provider Daily Summary - this report is a summary for the number of accepted claims per batch. This report also has a totals section which displays all input, accepted, and rejected daily.

Provider Monthly Summary - this report displays the number of accepted claims sent to the receivers including MTD and YTD. The second section of this report is a monthly summary and percentage listing of claim - level rejections and warnings.

Unprocessed Claims Report - this informs the provider that the following claims are unable to be processed by the payor and what corrective action should be taken.

Request for Additional Information - this report informs the provider that the following claims require additional information for processing. Each message identifies the information required to process the claims and the address to send the information.

Zero Payment Report - will list those claims for which the payor has determined no payment will be made.

INSURANCE PAYMENTS ARE OFTEN DELAYED BY:

Lost Claims

Rejected Claims

Manual Processing

Constant Change of Filing Regulations

We keep up on the latest changes and you see a faster return on your money!

~ WE WILL ~

Waive all set-up fees!

Electronically submit your claims!

Improve your cash flow!

Lower your operating costs!

Reduce your claim error rate!

Give you a faster return on your money!

~ AND ~
THE BOTTOM LINE
~
WE HAVE NO HIDDEN FEES!

CONSIDER A FEW STATISTICS:

- *Insurance companies and physicians bill over $3 billion annually processing paper claims. Doctors spend over $700 million in postage alone.*

- *Physicians generate over 3 billion claims each year (that's approximately 95 claims every second of every day).*

- *The industry average shows that an excess of 33% of insurance claims are suspended or rejected because of paper claim errors.*

- *Out of the total claims filed in this country annually, less than 10% are being processed electronically.*

NATIONAL STATISTICS:

PAPER CLAIMS VS. ELECTRONIC CLAIMS PROCESSING

	PAPER	ELECTRONIC
First-time rejection rate	30%	2%
Payment time	30 - 90 days	14- 21 days
Preparation time	Up to 15 min.	Many > 2 min.
Cost per claims	$ 8 - $10	$ 2 - $ 4
Advise of problems	After rejection	IMMEDIATE

*Statistics New England Journal of Medicine

COST OF FILING A PAPER CLAIM

Assume: 400 claims/month

Cost of Capital 10%

Salary of Insurance Clerk
(25% for benefits) . . . . $ 20,800 year

Average Claim . . . .$ 50.00

Rejection Rate 30%

* * * * * * * * *

Insurance Clerk	$ 4.33
Postage	.32
Forms - HCFA 1500 - @ .06 - Envelope @ .04	.10
Cost of Capital	.62
Rejected Claims Follow-up	.48
Cost of Capital Rejected Claims	.13
Billing to Patient (accepted)	1.50
Billing to Patient (rejected)	.75
TOTAL COST TO FILE A SINGLE CLAIM	**$ 8.23**

*Statistics New England Journal of Medicine

Chapter 18

The Presentation Packet

Let me say something about the presentation packet. You marketed the physician/dentist. You have already sent them a packet. Assuming they did their homework, the presentation is the icing on the cake.

The following pages are some examples I have used during my presentations. I place them in plastic page holders in a loose leaf binder or a flip chart purchased from A-PAPERS. I review these with the doctor, much the same way an insurance salesman does.

You are now at the presentation and like most other people you are nervous. The doctor/dentist has already received and reviewed your packet. By now he/she should have considerable knowledge and a good understanding of your services and the advantages of a billing service. Therefore, on your presentation day I can tell you not to be nervous, but I know you will be. Just realize that it won't be as bad as you anticipate it will be. You'll probably be nervous thinking that he/she may ask you questions you don't have answers to. Don't worry about that. Chances are it won't happen. If that does happen, simply tell him that you don't have an answer for him right now but you will call him in the morning and give him the answer.

When you get this far (actually meeting with the doctor), you are there to hopefully close the deal and negotiate a fee. Your packet information has informed the doctor and he now knows he needs outside resources

When you present to the doctor, you will flip through the binder describing and commenting to the doctor on information the doctor had already received. You are using your presentation pages as a guide to help keep your nerves intact and keep focused on what you want to say. In my experience, presentations go very quickly and you end up discussing where you are from, your background, possibly your experience and how you are going to pick up their claims or will they fax them to you. Presentation day is usually the icing to getting the account.

Just to show you how anyone can do a presentation I would like to share a true story with you. The first time I managed to get an appointment with a doctor I couldn't take off from my full-time job. I talked my husband (who was very supportive) in to going in my place which meant that he would be . . . alone. I briefed him the night before and called him that morning to give him support on what he should know and elaborated on each page of the presentation package. Bob is not the nervous kind and talking or presenting in a group doesn't bother him. He is in management with the FAA so he is used to this. However, this time he was a nervous wreck . . . but he was willing to help me. Off he went to the appointment as if he knew what he was talking about.

He apologized to the doctor that I was unable to make the appointment and that he was there on my behalf.

He was able to flip through the binder describing and commenting to the doctor on information the doctor had already received. When he was finished, the doctor had only a few questions which basically were how he would get the claims to us and my collection practice. My husband told him I would get back to him in the morning. IT WORKED! I had my first doctor and my husband helped me get him.

The following pages are examples of what I put into my presentation packet for my meeting with the doctor. Sometimes I use all of the pages and there are times when I only use a few of the pages. I feel that presentation pages are only a crutch to keep you focused and get your points across.

Also at the presentation you will need to know how you plan on getting their claims (fax, courier, pick-up, etc.). Usually the tiny details are worked out at that time. They may ask if you are to do full patient billing, who will get the patient phone calls regarding the bills, how often do you mail out patient statements, what reports will they get, your hours of operation, etc. You need to think through all the little details before your meeting.

Page 1

CLAIMS SUBMITTED WITH 97% ACCURACY RATE

In other words - - - the claims are made payable before they are submitted

Page 2

LESS COST

National average $8 - $10 per claim

Electronic submission can save you up to 50%

Page 3

LESS TIME . . .

NATIONAL AVERAGE

30-60-90 Days

ELECTRONIC SUBMISSION

14-21 days

Page 4 ➡

MORE MONEY...

National Average - Only

70% of Claims are Paid

*Electronic Submission
Average - 97%*

Customized Database

- *Provider Information*
- *Repeat Patient*
- *Insurance Companies*

*We only get this
information from you <u>once!</u>*

Page 5

⬅

Charges Customized For Your Office

You Only Pay For The Services You Need

Page 6 ➡

We Will Negotiate

"No One Is Too Big Or Too Small"

Page 7 ➡

> *Someday ALL healthcare claims will be processed electronically.*
>
> *It will save you time & money.*
>
> *Shouldn't you start saving that time & money*
>
> *TODAY?*
>
> "The money you save is yours, not the insurance company's. Invest your savings in your future."

Page 8 ➡ **INFO NEEDED FROM THE PHYSICIAN**

~ New and updated patient and insurance information
   (Super-Bill or Equivalent, HCFA 1500 signed by patient)
~ Insurance company name and policy/group number
   (Explanation of benefits, front/back of insurance card)
~ Diagnosis and procedure codes for each charge
~ Physicians fees for each service
   (Any form specific to the practice)
~ Any correspondence regarding billing or claim submission (carrier, patient, attorney, etc.)

NOTE: Super-bills may be faxed or mailed, unless other arrangements are made to be picked up weekly.

Additional Pages

~ *THE CLEARINGHOUSE* ~

We submit claims directly to the Clearinghouse which . . .

- *Retrieves all information within 24 hours via modem*

- *Sort, validate and check against updated editing criteria*

- *Reports any errors to us within 24 hours*

- *Will process and transmit to insurance carriers for payment*

- *Payment is made within 14-21 days*

~ BENEFITS ~

*Electronic filing will revolutionize your
claim submission practice by:*

➡ Increasing your cash flow with faster payment of claims

➡ Eliminating costly claim errors with computerized checking of claims

➡ Reducing your rejection/denial rate with eligibility and benefit verification

➡ Decreasing your billing costs and lowering your office overhead

~~~~~~

*By taking the headache of insurance claim
submission out of the office,
your staff will have more time to concentrate
on your patient's needs
and provide quality care*

Chapter 19

Contracts & Forms

You will talk to many people about contracts and you will get many different opinions. A contract is a binding agreement between you and the doctor. It will guarantee their business for a full year. On the other hand it will also guarantee the doctor your business and fee for a full year. What happens if you decide you don't want to do business with that doctor after a few months? Can you break the contract? You probably wouldn't want the hassle of going to court to break a contract, whereby he could easily take you to court for breaking the contract.

My opinion has changed greatly regarding contracts. Although I don't have any contracts in force at the present time, my new doctors will have a contract. My previous thoughts were if I am doing a good job and the doctor is happy with me then I don't have anything to worry about. I also felt that if I was not happy with him/her or their office staff, I wouldn't want to be locked into a binding agreement. Ideally you are looking for mutual benefits and satisfaction.

Since then my thoughts have changed radically on the subject of contracts. I think contracts are something you have to really think about. I negotiated with an internist with a patient database of roughly 1500 patients. During Christmas week, I drove an hour and a half each way to his office for three days and copied all his ledger cards. He was on vacation so I had the office to myself. Once I copied the cards, the tedious job of entering the data in my medical software began. I carried forward his patient balances. I was ready to begin work for him and excited about having the opportunity to have a big account. Only I didn't get the account. This situation will not happen to everyone but it should serve as a lesson learned. This particular doctor lost his hospital privileges and was having some sort of a nervous breakdown. His wife, the office manager, decided to hold off on letting me submit claims electronically. As of this writing, I don't know whether or not I will still get the account. If I do, I feel my time was not lost. However; the bottom line is, I had no contract and the 80 hours I devoted to him are lost. A contract would have allowed me to bill him for my time.

In the future, when I negotiate with a doctor I will be specific and waive all set-up fees. However, in the event I don't submit his/her claims because they changed their minds, **then they will be responsible for the set-up fee**. Speaking of set-up fee's . . . many billing centers charge a set-up fee for entering patient data. That is something only you can decide. However, I will continue not to charge a set-up fee, although you can be sure that if a deal like the one previously mentioned fell through, I will charge a set-up fee.

Other information to put in a contract is that they or you have 30 days to terminate. The reason I like that is because if I am having a problem with the doctor or his/her staff and I don't want to submit claims for them anymore, I don't want to be locked into a binding agreement for one year. I prefer the 30 days written notice, but then again, it is a matter of personal preference.

Electronic Medical Claims Contract

This agreement is to be effective between (Billing Center) and (Physician) on the _____ day of _____, 19__.

Both parties are in agreement to the following conditions:

1. (Billing Center) agrees to submit claims electronically for (Provider) or drop to paper when needed after receipt from doctor's office (often within 48 hours).

2. (Billing Center) will provide a monthly report(s) to (Provider).

3. (Billing Center) agrees that no collection action will be taken with a patient unless discussed with Provider.

4. (Billing Center) is waiving all set-up fee's; however, in the event that (Billing Center) inputs all patient data from (Provider) and (Provider) voids this contract, (Provider) is responsible for the hourly rate which (Billing Center) consumed from imputing patient data, not to exceed $500.

5. (Provider) agree to pay _____ dollars for (Billing Center) monthly fees. These rates may change after one year. Payment will be made within 30 days.

6. This agreement shall be for one year and will be automatically renewed for an additional year at the date of expiration; however, it is understood that (Billing Center) or (Provider) may terminate this agreement upon a thirty (30) day written notice.

_____   _____
(Billing Center)   (Provider)

Medical Claims Submission Agreement

This agreement, between **Your billing center**, an electronic medical claims billing center, located in **Your Town, Your State and Provider Name** on this ____ day of _____,199-__ is a Medical Claims Submission agreement.

We agree to the following:

1. **Billing center name** will pick up claims information from provider/or the provider will mail/fax claims on ____ unless other arrangements have been made, and both parties have agreed.

2. **Billing center name** will provide audit entry information from submitted claims to provider on a monthly basis unless other arrangements have been made and both parties have agreed.

3. **Provider Name** agrees to pay ____ dollars ($__) per claim submitted. **Provider Name** will be billed on the ____ day of each month. Payment of these charges shall be made with (30) days. These rates may change after one year as agreed upon by both parties.

4. The term of this agreement shall be for one (1) year and shall be automatically renewed for an additional year at the date of expiration. **Billing center name** and **Provider Name** agree that this Agreement may be terminated by either party upon submission of a thirty (30) day written notice.

Your Billing Center name   Provider Name

By _____   By _____

Service Agreement

This agreement is made by and between **Billing Center Name** and **Provider Name** on this ___ day of _____, 19__.

The parties hereto agree as follows:

1.0 CLAIMS PROCESSING SERVICES

1.1 **Billing Center Name** will pick up claims information from **Provider Name.**

1.2 **Billing Center Name** will electronically process and submit **Provider's Name** claims to the corresponding insurance companies and provide a computer-generated report verifying their receipt by the insurance companies. The claims will be processed within two business days, excluding those claims that contain errors.

1.3 **Billing Center Name** or Clearinghouse will process those claims that cannot be transmitted electronically and mail them to the corresponding insurance companies.

2.0 COMPENSATION

2.1 **Provider Name** agrees to pay **Billing Center Name** for the services described in section 1 at the rate of ___ of the total claims submitted monthly. **Billing Center Name** will invoice provider at the beginning of each month for the previous month and attach to the invoice a confirmation report from the clearinghouse. Remittance of these charges will be due in full within 30 days.

3.0 TERMS of AGREEMENT

3.1 This agreement may be terminated by either party upon the submission of a thirty (30) days written notice.

This agreement has been executed this day and year first written above.

REPRESENTATIVE FOR BILLING CENTER   DATE
REPRESENTATIVE FOR PROVIDER   DATE

Physician/Patient Information Sheet

The following are examples of a Physician Information and a Patient Information sheet. Again, you may need to adjust them for your specific needs. The Physician sheet will save you time since you will have all the information at your finger tips. The Patient Information sheet is a sheet to use if you are signing on a "new" doctor who has no forms in their office.

I find most doctors today have a Patient Information sheet in their office already and to get them to change their form to use yours would be quite difficult. Doctors and their staff are set in their ways and changes are always hard for them. People are actually afraid of change and even though it is a small thing like a patient information sheet, they generally prefer to use what they have.

However, always make sure that the physician has a "signature on file" for the patient. It is critical in filing insurance claims and it is better to be on the safe side.

PHYSICIAN INFORMATION SHEET

PRACTICE NAME_____

ADDRESS_____

CITY_____STATE_____ZIP _____

PHONE#_____FAX#_____

PHYSICIAN NAME_____

OFFICE CONTACT PERSON _____

FEDERAL TAX ID / SS #_____UPIN # _____

MEDICARE #_____

MEDICAID #_____

BLUE CROSS/BLUE SHIELD #_____

OTHER NUMBERS _____

PATIENT INFORMATION SHEET

NAME _____
ADDRESS _____
CITY _____ STATE _____ ZIP _____
HOME PHONE _____ WORK PHONE _____
EMPLOYER: _____
PERSON TO CONTACT IN CASE OF EMERGENCY: _____
_____ RELATIONSHIP _____
PHONE _____
SPOUSE _____ WORK PHONE _____
REFERRING DOCTOR _____

INSURANCE INFORMATION

NAME OF INSURED _____
ADDRESS _____
TELEPHONE # _____

Insurance Type: Medicare [ ]   Medicaid [ ]   BC/BS[ ]
                 Workers Comp [ ]   Other [ ]
Policy # _____ Group # _____
If other, name of Insurance Company_____

SECONDARY INSURANCE COMPANY_____
Policy # _____ Group # _____

Have you met your deductible?   Yes [ ] No [ ]
Do you have a co-payment for office visits? Yes [ ] No [ ]
If yes, how much? ____

Whom may we thank for your visit here today?
_____

Thank you for taking the time to complete this information.
All records are strictly confidential.

CHAPTER 20

SOFTWARE AND ITS COST

How much does it cost?
Where do I buy software?
What kind of software do I buy?
Do I need software?

When I first went into business, my husband felt I should have a doctor lined up before I purchased software. Being as impetuous as I am, I wanted software first, doctor second. I reasoned that I could not learn the business fully if I didn't have the software. So I won the argument, spent $4,000, and had my software. Four months later I landed my first doctor and it was time to use my software. I spent eight frustrating days trying to learn my new software. It was the most complicated, most difficult, unbelievable software out there and to think - I thought I did my homework on buying software. *I purchased software that was useless.* I felt like quitting before starting. The software was not user friendly like I was told, it was not easy, it was not anything like what I thought. The book was not even updated.

The software salesman (and partner in his own clearinghouse) came and spent two days training me. The two days consisted of several hours of software training, marketing, reviewing the manual and several hours of trying to get the software to transmit to his clearinghouse. What did I know!!!! Since then, I've come a long way and learned that there are a lot of software vendors out there who use this same approach.

After two weeks, I submitted my first batch of claims and thought this was great. I finally did it. It heighten my esteem to think I worked my way through this complicated mess. What I didn't know is that the batch sat in this particular clearinghouse and was never tested or submitted to Medicare/Medicaid. Finally after 2 months of tears and frustration I called Medicare and found out they were never submitted. I didn't know that this clearinghouse/vendor was not approved in my state and therefore I could not submit my claims electronically. I called my clearinghouse and learned they were using my claims as test claims. No one ever told me. Then I found out that even though they were to be test claims, someone slipped up and FORGOT about them. They were never submitted. The clearinghouse didn't even report back to me any errors on claims submitted like they promised to do. I was at the point now where I had to face my doctor and explain to him why his claims, which I promised him would have a turnaround of 14-21 days, were still not processed after 60 days.

I thought I would go crazy. My mind was racing and I felt like sending everything back to the doctor, never seeing him again, and saying good-bye to the business. Yes, I was ready to quit. Only I kept thinking that I can't be a quitter, especially with all the money I had invested. I would have also have to face my family and friends. I would have to continue forward and endure whatever came back. Thankfully, my doctor was understanding and we worked out a mutual agreement. I didn't have the heart to charge him until I had the proper software and patient accounting to handle his account the way I had initially promised. I worked his claims for eight months at no cost.

Then came the time to do "Patient Accounting." I used Lotus, I used Excel. I even purchased an accounting system. I would try anything anyone suggested but was hesitant to buy new software, nor did I have the money. Finally I realized I needed medical software that had patient accounting functions, and to do the entire job properly I would need a clearinghouse. You have to spend money sometimes to make money. Many people have tried the same method, one type of medical software, another type of accounting system and needless to say they are not compatible. The result is repetitive data entry for the same patient, multiplied by many patients will take weeks to accomplish. I learned the hard way as many other medical billing entrepreneurs have experienced, and now are out of business.

The bottom line of this story is don't be fooled like I was. There are many, and I mean many, software vendors out there. You will actually get dizzy. Most of these vendors state the same thing, I have the best, the most advanced, the most user friendly. Yeah, right!!!! You are ready to buy software and you don't want to make a mistake and you also want the best deal. The harsh reality is that many of these software vendors don't care about you, just your money. They are not there to help you with your business, and you are soon all alone. And that brings me to **the bottom line** . . . be careful with the software you purchase and who you purchase it from. You may need future support! Where will they be? Did you ever buy a computer or appliance, etc., have a problem and call the store back? What did they tell you? Call service. They were not there to help you with your problem.

Some big software companies buy software (ex.; MediSoft) and package it for over $6,000. The software cost them $499, they throw in some marketing and software training, and also some video tapes. They may fly you to California or New York, you stay for 2 or 3 days, and spend two days training. You feel like you are really in business now because you spent a lot of money to get this far. Did you learn medical billing? The software/marketing firm sends you home to begin your new business. Finally the reality of the $6,000 (or more) sinks in your brain and you find out you could have saved the $6,000 plus and purchased software for less. What did you know? Their brochures were enticing and elaborately done. Don't let the packages you see advertised fool you. These big time sales people advertise in *USA Today, Home Business*, etc. You don't have to spend all that money to get involved in the business. Buy from someone that is reputable, that you know you can trust. Sales people are high pressured and swift talkers. BE AWARE!.

A lot of these big companies are also under FTC investigation. You need to be very very careful. Is it worth $6,000 to fly somewhere, spend 2 nights in a hotel or would you rather save your money and put it into marketing? As a MediSoft dealer I have to admit I'm prejudiced towards MediSoft.

Networking on Prodigy was my biggest inspiration. There, I met Jo-Anne Sheehan and Bruce Wade. Joanne, my biggest mentor, has a successful medical business billing center in Massachusetts. Jo-Anne started in her home and now has a beautiful suite and bills for over 40 physicians. Without Jo-Anne's help and inspiration, I would have quit when I had purchased the useless software. Once again, I became motivated because of Jo-Anne and I cannot leave out Bruce Wade from Alabama who guided me with Medisoft and kept telling me I could do it, I just needed decent software. Bruce is a special person.

The bottom line . . . when you're ready to buy software, make sure it is from a reputable dealer and that you have a reputable clearinghouse. You will not only save time, but you will also save money. More food for thought. I recommend buying from a software vendor who has experience in the billing business as well. How can a salesperson sell you software when they don't use it, and they can't answer your questions about it? They are programmed only in selling the software. Would you buy a computer from a salesperson who never used a computer before? Well, software is much the same way. Someone who has used the software and knows it inside and out can understand the problems you may encounter, and can give you the support you deserve. There are a lot of vendors out there who don't operate a billing center, they only sell software or software and a marketing package. When you have a problem and can't figure out how to do actual billing, are they going to be able to help you?

When this book was first written I had a list of software vendors; however, as the final printing day approached I decided not to list them. In the two years it took me to write this book I learned a lot from people all over the country, although having been trained at other training centers, still called me because they did not have a solid basic understanding of medical billing. therefore, I decided not to endorse of list any company and formed The Academy of Medical Billing in partnership with Jo-Anne Sheehan.

The Academy saw the growing need for qualified medical billers in the healthcare industry. Undoubtedly, you too have seen business opportunities available where you can purchase software and marketing training for exorbitant costs. As experts in the industry, Jo-Anne and I have spoken to many people who have made the big investment, yet still felt unqualified to market a service they did not understand. The Academy of Medical billing wants you to succeed, whether it be as a third party biller in a medical group practice or on your own as an entrepreneur. We want you to see the vision . . . The Vision of Success!

At the Academy you will see first hand how a medical billing service operates. The Academy of Medical billing is one of the country's first training centers in a medical billing office. Besides our basic medical billing course, we also offer you MediSoft software and training, marketing training for a medical billing service and an informal forum after training where you can meet a doctor and discuss real billing concerns.

There are several training options available to you. Call 1-800-221-0488 for the latest package. When you leave the academy, you will be prepared and knowledgeable in the insurance industry. We are not offering a business opportunity. Our primary focus is in medical billing and we cover marketing, software and give you a solid background to sell a service.

Clearinghouses - The Big Question?

What is a clearinghouse? Why do I need to use a clearinghouse? I could save money and submit claims directly or on paper! Those questions are the most asked questions I've ever heard.

Let's begin by explaining what a clearinghouse is. Believe it or not a clearinghouse can be the size of your living room, it can be a room size of an 8' x 8'. Whatever the size, visualize a room full of computers. You modem your claim to a computer and that computer downloads your claim into the specific insurance carriers format. Unfortunately many carriers have different formats. Once your claim is formatted, the clearinghouse then transmits that claim directly to the insurance carrier and your money is on its way.

How about the life of a paper claim? As you can see by the diagram on the following page, a paper claim has a long life. When you submit to a clearinghouse you immediately get a acceptance /rejection notice on your computer screen. If your claim is accepted, it means that it is on its way to the proper insurance carrier. Submitting electronically saves you the costly expense of paying for postage, envelopes and saves time. The general rule is the claim submitted to a clearinghouse is accepted and will be paid in approximately 7 - 10 days.

When the claim is rejected on your computer screen you then have the opportunity to open that particular claim and fix the problem. Most clearinghouses will allow you to fix a claim on screen which means that you have a list of names on your screen with accept/reject. You click on the reject and up comes your claim. The area which is being rejected is highlighted. It may be for a missing area code,

130   MEDICAL BILLING: THE BOTTOM LINE

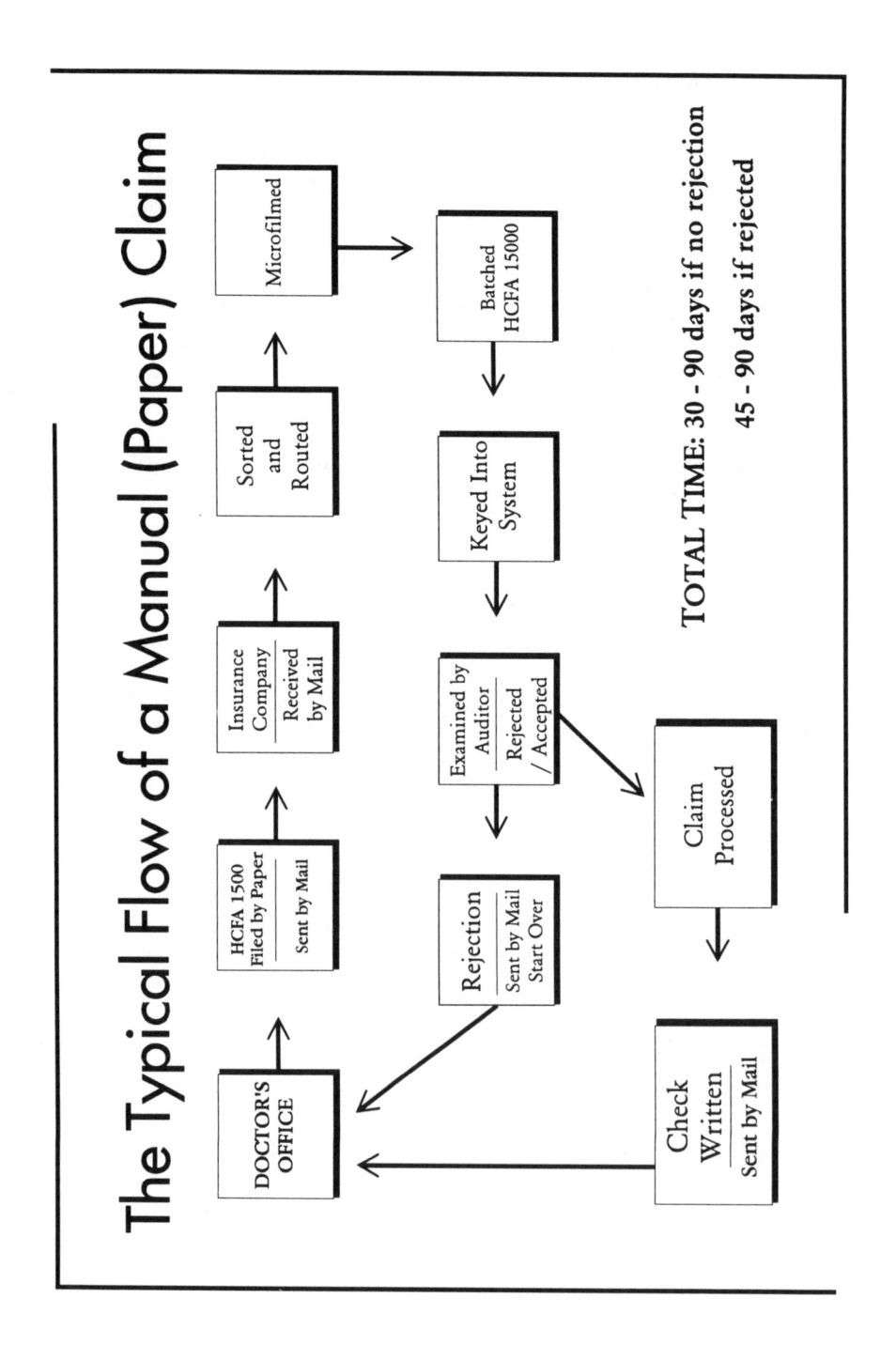

The Typical Flow of a Manual (Paper) Claim

DOCTOR'S OFFICE → HCFA 1500 Filed by Paper / Sent by Mail → Insurance Company Received by Mail → Sorted and Routed → Microfilmed

→ Batched HCFA 15000 → Keyed Into System → Examined by Auditor Rejected / Accepted

→ Rejection Sent by Mail Start Over (back to Doctor's Office)

→ Claim Processed → Check Written Sent by Mail (back to Doctor's Office)

TOTAL TIME: 30 - 90 days if no rejection
45 - 90 days if rejected

birthdate, wrong HIC number, or sex is missing. Whatever the rejection, you have the opportunity of fixing it and sending it back.

If on the other hand, the rejection is because the procedure code and diagnosis codes do not match (ex: suture removal as a procedure code/diabetes as a diagnostic code) then you can either get the patients superbill and fix the error or call the physicians office and get the proper diagnosis or procedure.

A clearinghouse will sort, validate and check against extensive, and continuously updated editing criteria to insure accuracy and completeness of claims. This is done before they are sent electronically to the insurance carriers.

When I started out I didn't use a clearinghouse. Now that I use a clearinghouse, I cannot tell you how much my life has changed utilizing the benefits of the clearinghouse. There are many clearinghouses out there. Because I live in New Hampshire I have the opportunity to use Stat Link which is for New Hampshire providers only.

Do your homework! I've listed a partial list of clearinghouses you can contact. Talk to other billing centers in your state, get on-line, network and find out what is the best clearinghouse around. Clearinghouses change rapidly. More and more companies are getting into the clearinghouse business and more and more companies are getting out. You need to shop for a clearinghouse like you do for software.

132 MEDICAL BILLING: THE BOTTOM LINE

This is a partial list

	HCA	Dental	UB92	Paper	Set-Up Fee	Per Claim Fee	Audit/Edit Report
EQUIFAX HEALTHCARE EDI 1854 Shackelord Ct Ste 200 Norcross, GA 30093 800-882-0802 (fax 404-806-4799)	YES	YES	YES	YES	300	0.47	Immediate
MEDICAL DATA PROCESSING 555 Oakbrook Pkwy Suite 365 Norcross, GA 30093 404-368-1993 (fax 404-368-4067)	YES			NO	NO	0.35	Immediate
AT&T 12402 Industrial Blvd. #A8 Victorville, CA 92392 619-955-1788 (fax 619-955-1789)	YES	YES	?	YES	NO	0.35	45 Minutes
INTEGRATED MEDICAL SYSTEMS 17050 Bushard St Ste 300 Fountain Valley, CA 92708 714-964-9965 (fax 714-965-9417)	YES	NO			250	.25-.35	Not Immediate
ENVOY 2708 Alternate 19N Ste 501 Palm Harbor, FL 34683 800-735-6277 (fax 813-784-5493)	YES	YES	YES	YES	100	0.4	Not Immediate
SOFTWARE DEPOT 239 New Road Parsippany NJ 07054 201-244-0003 or 800-753-3768	YES	YES	YES	YES	49	.25-.35	Not Immediate
EIS -800-576-6412		YES			50	.50	Not Known

Names, addresses and fees are subject to change.
Author holds no guarantee.

Seminars to Inquire About:

The Academy of Medical Billing -	800-221-0488
CAY Medical Management -	603-465-6062
National Assoc. of Claims Proff.-	800-660-0665
Communications Group -	800-929-4824
Medical Management Institute-	800-334-5724
Medicode Coding Seminar-	800-899-4600
Inpact Medical Consulting-	800-252-9094

Mailing Lists (Physicians not filing electronically)

CAY Medical Management   800-221-0488

Organizations/Newsletters

The Academy of Medical Billing
PO Box 39
N. Reading, MA 01864
800-221-0488

NACAP - 1-708-963-3500
National Association of Claims
Assistance Professionals
4724 Florence Avenue
Downers Grove, Illinois 60515

Medicode - 800-999-4600
5225 Wiley Post Way
Ste 500
Salt Lake City, Utah 84116

Hot Topics - 602-944-9877
7803 N. 12th Avenue
Phoenix, Arizona 85021

The Post Office has a program called "Zip + 4 Diskette Coding". They clean up mailing lists created in Windows and DOS, making them more accurate and putting them in a form that's easier for mail handlers to sort and cheaper for you to send. You become eligible for their bar-code discount should you decide to add them to your mailers. You need an application which takes about a month. This will also eliminate mail which is returned for "Attempt Not Known," "Deceased," etc. Check with your post office to get more details.

Database Marketing

For less than $300 you can own Select Phone and Microsoft Access 2.0. Select Phone allows you to search by SIC code in a number of ways. (Then you can export it in, access and make any changes or corrections.) It is a simple process. You can then do your phone survey and separate the doctors who are filing electronically from those who are not. Use this information for mailing labels, which Access creates automatically and a host of other items. Buy WinFax Pro 4.0 ($79.) and export the database's to it from Access. Then create a flyer and FAX away for free. For Select Phone you will need a CD Rom, and to run Access properly you will need at least a 486 with 6 meg of Ram and a roomy hard drive.

NEIC
500 Plaza Drive
Secaucus, New Jersey 07094
800-877-0004

MEDICARE
Call your local Medicare office and get on their list.

St. Anthony's
800-632-0123
Order their newsletter

CHAPTER 21

CLARIFYING THE ALPHABET SOUP OF MANAGED CARE

Part of the frustration of dealing with managed care comes from the abundance of new and unfamiliar terms and ACRONYMS used to describe it. Here is a handy summary of some terms that will shed some light on what is involved in managed care.

WHAT IS CAPITATION?

Capitation is a fixed payment, in advance, to a provider on a per-member basis, regardless of the number of services provided to each member. Rates can be adjusted based on demographics or projected medical cost.

WHAT IS MEDIGAP?

Medigap is a secondary insurance, which when filed electronically to Medicare, will be forwarded to the patient's secondary insurance if they are receiving electronic claims submissions.

What is Managed Care?

Managed care is an umbrella term for any system that integrates financing and delivery of appropriate medical care by means of:

- Contracts with selected physicians and hospitals that furnish a comprehensive set of health care to enrolled members, usually for a predetermined monthly premium.
- Has utilization and quality controls that providers agree to accept.
- Provides financial incentives for patients to use providers and facilities association with the plan.
- Required assumption of some financial risk by doctors.

What is a Primary Care Physician?

A primary care physician (PCP) is a patients primary doctor. In a managed care setting you cannot go to a specialist unless your PCP recommends a specialist. If you do decide to go to another doctor without a recommendation, you are responsible for the payment and chances are your insurance will not pay for it.

What is a Gatekeeper?

A gatekeeper is a primary care physician, usually a family physician, general practitioner, internist, osteopath or pediatrician. HMO's often will not pay for services not approved by gatekeepers, who must authorize medical services, elective hospitalizations, referrals and diagnostic work-ups.

What is an HMO (Health Maintenance Organization)?

An HMO is an organized system of care that provides health care services to a defined population for per-person fee. Members are not reimbursed for care not provided or authorized by the HMO.

WHAT IS A PREFERRED PROVIDE LIST?

A list of providers with reputations for quality and efficiency, compiled by an employer for its employees. These providers have no contracts with the employer, and no financial incentives are offered to employees to choose them.

WHAT IS A CO-PAYMENT?

A co-payment is a form of cost sharing in which an HMO member makes a nominal payment to a provider at the time of service, typically for office visits and prescription drugs.

WHAT IS CO-INSURANCE?

Percentage of cost of care paid by patients as part of insurance coverage?

WHAT IS CASE MANAGEMENT?

Case management is a concurrent evaluation of the necessity, appropriateness or efficiency of services and drugs provided to patients on a case-by-case basis, usually targeted at potentially high-cost cases.

WHAT IS A DEDUCTIBLE?

A deductible is a set dollar amount beneficiaries must pay toward covered charges before insurance coverage can begin. Usually renewed annually.

Chapter 22

Common Questions & Answers

How much does it cost to get started?

In some states you can start for as little as zero dollars with your state's Medicare/Medicaid software. Other states charge for using their software or you can order for $99. MediSoft or Lytec starter package, get familiar with software, and then decide which software or upgrade you really need. Using your state's software may not be compatible with your software and it would be double entry. Very few states have compatible software so you will need to buy an interface.

What should I do first to start my business?

Write a marketing plan (and see how much money you can afford to put into marketing). Then get postcards made up and test your market and see what your response is. If you are getting a response, think about software. In the meantime call Medicare/Medicaid and see if they have free software for your state. As previously discussed, you may want full patient accounting software, therefore you will need to purchase the software from a reputable software vendor. Once you decide you can do this business, take the plunge and buy software.

WHO SHOULD I TARGET IN ON?

My personal opinion is to begin targeting in on chiropractors, podiatrist, ambulance companies, and psychiatrists. They generally are not part of a huge group or an HMO/PPO. They tend to have small practices and do their own billing or hire an outside billing center to help them. A larger practice may be too much to handle in the beginning until you have your software and patient accounting down firm. Remember, this is my personal opinion only.

SHOULD I SPEND THE MONEY ON A SEMINAR?

Absolutely, the networking and knowledge you will gain can save you money in the long run.

SHOULD I ORDER BOOKS RIGHT AWAY?

To start I recommend purchasing *Understanding Medical Insurance, A Step-by-Step Guide* by Joanne Rowell, as previously mentioned in the reference section. This book will give you general knowledge of insurance forms, how they are to be filled out, and the step-by-step process of an insurance claim. You will also need a current ICD 9-CM and CPT book to file claims.

WHAT SHOULD I SAY IN MY PRESENTATION?

You have a presentation package. Use that package and keep it simple. Don't oversell, don't undersell. Don't forget the doctor already has a lot of information about your service. Just know how you will pick up the claims, your fee schedule, and give him a sheet about what he can expect from your office and what you can expect from his office.

CAN I BILL FOR A DENTAL OFFICE?

Dental claims don't use ICD9-CM codes and the x-rays are not required for post-procedures today. They can be asked for in a post-payment audit though. All preauthorizations can be submitted electronically if you have the correct software. Lytec and MediSoft allow dental billing.

WHEN I BUY MY BILLING SOFTWARE PACKAGE, WHAT TRAINING MIGHT I EXPECT TO RECEIVE AND HOW LONG CAN I RECEIVE SUPPORT FROM THE COMPANY?

Some companies will sell you the software and say good-bye. The price you pay has nothing to do with the bottom line. Investigate the various software companies and learn of their reputation, preferably through other users and associations. As far as continuing informational support and software upgrades, again, get information on various companies reputations.

WHO CAN I TALK TO ABOUT THE BUSINESS - HOW CAN I REACH PEOPLE?

Use your computer, get on line with the internet, Prodigy, CompuServe, America-On-Line. Network — network — network! A reputable software dealer will give you names of other dealers and entrepreneurs. Do a press release in your local newspapers and try to advertise in the AMA Newsletter in your state.

ONCE I HAVE MY SOFTWARE, MUST I DEAL WITH A CLEARINGHOUSE AND IF SO, WHAT IS THE COST?

The cost will vary. No, you don't have to deal with a Clearinghouse but it is highly advisable. The cost involved would be cost per claim, new provider sign on cost, yearly fees, etc. You shouldn't have to buy any additional software.

IS THE BUSINESS PRETTY WELL LOCKED UP BY MOST PROVIDERS BEING SERVICED ALREADY?

My personal opinion is that it is still a wide open market. We are in the beginning stages with the advent of healthcare reform and new regulations which I believe will require or force providers to file electronically. Bankers and airline companies have already been conducting business electronically for years and eventually the whole medical industry will follow. It saves money and time, causing increased productivity.

How do I advertise?

Word of mouth, referrals, cold calling, marketing with letters, postcards and brochures. AMA newsletters, local hospitals.

If I don't succeed, can I get a refund?

Most companies do not have a refund policy. Think carefully, is this business for you?

Do I need previous experience?

Having no experience is not a factor. Of course if you have some business or medical experience, this may be an advantage. Otherwise the information to succeed is out there, as described in this manual and other publications. The will and desire to learn and persevere are the secrets to most new ventures. However, you can gain tremendous experience at The Academy of Medical Billing.

What is the overall cost to start my business?

That depends on what you are budgeting. You need to take into consideration the software costs and marketing. Again, marketing needs to be persistent and consistent and you need to budget and follow up with marketing every week.

I am planning on retiring, is there an age limit?

Absolutely not, as a matter of fact you can probably take the business with you or sell it.